POLLARD

THE
SPY'S
STORY

THE
SPY'S
STORY

By
Bernard R. Henderson

ALPHA BOOKS
NEW YORK, N.Y.

ISBN: 0-944392-00-8

Printed in the United States of America

Produced by Madison Publishing Associates

Designed by Stanley S. Drate/Folio Graphics Co., Inc.

CONTENTS

POLLARD

THE SPY'S STORY

INTRODUCTION

On March 4, 1987, Jonathan Jay Pollard was sentenced to life imprisonment for giving Israel information classified secret by the United States government. At the same time, his wife, Anne Henderson Pollard, was given two five-year terms for "conspiring to receive" and "possessing" some of the "stolen property" (documents) he had secreted in their apartment.

Within days after his arrest in late November 1985, the government of Israel admitted having copies of the documents and agreed to return them to the United States, thus furnishing the evidence necessary for Jonathan Pollard's conviction. Prime Minister Peres apologized to the United States, but said the Jonathan Pollard operation was unauthorized by the Israeli government.

Anne Henderson Pollard was arrested a day later than her husband and accused of spying for China. Newspapers like *The New York Times* noted she was the second major suspect apprehended that year for selling secret information to the Chinese government. Magazines like *Time* pictured her alongside the Walkers, Pelton, and Chin and her husband as one of the spies caught in "The Year of the Spy."

Because of the severity of the charge, Anne Pollard was held in isolated detention without bail, as was her husband. She was released after ninety-five days in detention in severe physical condition from a combination of gastrointestinal and biliary disorders, which had gone untreated or poorly treated during her incarceration. She had lost forty pounds, and her hair—at age twenty-five—had begun to turn gray.

Jonathan Pollard was held in isolation for a year and a half until his sentencing, also undergoing severe physical and mental debilitation.

One of the first steps in the prosecution of the Pollards was to convene a grand jury in Washington. That grand jury considered various indictable offenses under United States espionage statutes. Those offenses are generally divided between the more serious charge of spying against the United States for an enemy (treason) and the lesser offense of spying for a friendly nation. Ultimately the grand jury indicted Jonathan Pollard for the lesser offense, spying for a friendly nation, there being no evidence of his spying for an enemy.

Anne Henderson Pollard was never indicted by the grand jury, since there was no evidence that she had been part of any espionage operation either for China or for Israel. However in a plea-bargain agreement with the prosecutors, she agreed to plead guilty to two minor charges—both involving her "receipt" or "possession" of documents found in the apartment—in return for a promise that sentences, if any, for these minor offenses would run concurrently. She was told by the prosecutors that unless she signed a guilty plea, the prosecutors would demand a life sentence for her husband. However, if she pleaded guilty, they would guarantee leniency for him. At the time, Anne Pollard was adamantly opposed to pleading guilty to any crime. However she was pressured by her attorney, James Hibey, and her father, Bernard Henderson, into making the plea, in their belief that the judge would recognize the triviality of the charges against her. In the end, she agreed because of her deep love for her husband and the promise of leniency for him.

As part of the plea-bargain agreement, signed in June 1986, both Pollards agreed to give their full cooperation to investigators from various intelligence agencies as well as the FBI. As a result of hundreds of hours of Jonathan Pollard's polygraphed testimony, the evidence furnished by Israel, and the unchallenged testimony in Israel by Israeli-government employees, the United States government named four Israelis as part of the espionage conspiracy: General Aviem Sella, a much-decorated Israeli pilot and war hero; Rafael Eitan, direct aide to Prime Minister Peres and Israel's legendary spy master (he had captured Adolf Eichmann); Yosuf Yagur, head of an Israeli "technical" mission in the United States; and Irit Erb, a secretary at the Israeli embassy in Washington. Once again, the U.S. government did not say Anne Pollard was part of the operation; in fact, she was never mentioned in the documents describing the conspiracy. Instead, as stated in the plea-bargain agreement, they admitted she had never passed documents to any foreign national.

JONATHAN POLLARD'S STORY

As the documents in this book indicate, Jonathan Jay Pollard is a dedicated Zionist; that is, he believes that the Jewish people should have a national homeland, Israel, and that people of Jewish descent (Diasporic Jews) have a moral obligation to insure the security of that homeland.

This belief differs somewhat from the loyalty of other Americans to the lands from which their ancestors came. Many Americans actively support organizations that foster cultural identification with lands of their origin. New York's and other cities' many parades, festivals, and fund-raising activities on behalf of the Irish, Italians, Poles, Greeks, Chinese, Hispanics, and dozens of other ethnic or national groups are powerful testimony to that fact. All of these people share a dual concern: love and pride in the United States and love and pride in their ancestral homelands.

However, what makes this different from the Jew's passionate concern for his homeland is that Israel was only recently established—and that as a result of the Holocaust—and exists under the most precarious of circumstances. The tiny nation of Israel is only the size of New Jersey and is surrounded by nations dedicated to its extermination.

Jonathan Pollard's family was personally involved in the Holocaust, seventy-five members of their Lithuanian relatives having died in death camps. As a child, he had traveled with his father to those then-silent camps and vowed he would never stand idly by if such threats were to surface again. His mother's brother, commander of an army hospital in Paris after World War II, had donated medical supplies and boots to the new Israeli army. His father, a renowned microbiologist, had received four Presidential citations for his work on antibodies during World War II, in which he injected himself in order to speed up their safety tests.

As Jonathan Pollard explains in his eloquent memorandum to the court (the censored copy of which is included in this book), the circumstances in which he found himself in 1984 caused him enormous emotional conflict. As a naval intelligence analyst possessing higher-than-secret clearance, he was aware of information collected by various United States intelligence branches that he believed was critical to Israel's survival. Although the United States and Israel have agreed to share secret information, much of that information was, in fact, being withheld. Whether, as Defense Secretary Caspar Weinberger argued, that was being done to insure that Israel was not too strong in relation to its Arab neighbors or whether it was simply low-level bureaucratic anti-Semitism as Pollard believes, is a matter for the reader to decide. In any event, CIA head William Casey had issued a directive in 1983 calling for full exchange of classified information with Israel on Middle Eastern matters.

The United States government has carefully censored out much of the court testimony regarding the information Pollard furnished Israel. However, by combining the statements that remain with later news disclosures, one can arrive at certain obvious conclusions.

First, Pollard gave the Israelis only that information which the United States obtained through its own spy apparatus in the Soviet Union and various Arab-allied nations. His polygraphed statements indicate that his agreement with Israel excluded any information regarding United States defenses. Prosecution testimony to the court contains phrases such as "might have," "could possibly have," "might possibly conclude," as speculations as to whether or not Israel could have learned any fact about United States defenses (assuming they did not already know it as part of regular information exchanges). However, nothing of a factual nature exists to indicate Israel learned anything new about United States defenses, or for that matter, that they wanted to learn it.

Those polygraphed statements also reveal that Pollard refused to give Israel the names of United States agents there (which Eitan did ask for) or in the neighboring Arab countries. It should be no surprise to the reader that all nations systematically spy on friend and enemy alike, and, considering the importance of any nation's security, they would be remiss if they did not do so. In 1987, Senator David Durenberger revealed the existence of United States agents in Israel, and was immediately chastised by his colleagues in the Senate. In addition, Pollard refused to give Eitan the United States personal files on Israeli leaders, which, as all people in any intelligence service know, contain hearsay regarding any immorality of which these people may be suspected, as well as psychological profiles. It is possible that Eitan wanted those files to foster his personal political power in Israel by blackmail; they were certainly never part of an Israeli government request.

One thing the testimony, documents, and newspaper reports do reveal is the tremendous sophistication of modern American intelligence gathering. The old methods of dependence on agents alone is gone forever. Today United States satellites can picture a man's face or read a license plate. Electronic interceptors can capture and decode messages anywhere in the world. And modern, high-speed computers can sort and classify millions of bits of data collected daily.

It is comforting to realize that not only does the United States know every technical detail about every current Russian weapons system and its associated electronic controls, but also all the details about weapons systems still under development.

It was less comforting to Pollard to realize that Israel had little such knowledge and that an impending crisis was brewing. In the period from 1983 to 1985, the Soviet Union and certain Arab-allied countries were rapidly changing the balance of power in the Middle East. Israel knew Iraq was building a nuclear plant capable of producing weapons-grade by-products. So was Pakistan. Israel destroyed the Iraqi plant in an air raid led by then-Colonel Sella. They knew Iraq had built gas plants and was poisoning its Irani enemy. However, Israel did not know that Syria had constructed a number of nerve-gas plants with equipment purchased from West Germany and was planning to use nerve gas on the Golan Heights. When Pollard asked why that information wasn't given to the Israelis, his superior explained that "Jews are too nervous about gas."

The most serious threat was being mounted by Syria in conjunction with other nations whose names have been deleted from Pollard's memorandum by government censors. The Syrian armed forces were being modernized with new-model Russian planes and missiles, including surface-to-air missiles, air-to-surface missiles, and surface-to-surface missiles. Although Israel was equipped with late-model American airplanes equivalent to the Soviet planes, it had little defense against the missiles, since it had limited knowledge of the electronic systems which guide and shield them. In other words, Israeli planes were vulnerable to Soviet-Syrian surface-to-air missiles while Israeli missiles lacked the electronic control capability to get through the electronic defenses of the Soviet missiles.

When Pollard asked his superiors why they were not giving the Israelis that information for the surface-to-air missiles, he was told that Jews were smart enough to learn the electronics after they lost a few planes. But an equally serious potential problem was the surface-to-surface missiles, able to hit Tel Aviv within seven minutes from any point in Syria. These missiles, which were being armed with nerve gas, could have devastated the Israeli population.

Still another concern of Pollard in this period was the exchange of information regarding terrorists, of which Israelis were the leading but not the only target. He says the roots of his decision to aid Israel went back to 1983 when bureaucratic delays made the bombing of the United States Marine Compound in Lebanon possible and Reagan's decision to "take the blame" swept under the rug the fact that American intelligence knew about the perpetrators and their location. Later incidents in which Jews were targets of terrorist acts reinforced that decision.

It has been well publicized that Pollard gave Israel detailed information which facilitated Israel's air strike against the PLO headquarters in Tunis, October 1, 1985. In addition to the Libyan antiaircraft deployment, he gave details of the PLO antiaircraft installations in Tunis. President Reagan at first lauded the Israeli strike as well he might, since the terrorist organization meeting there known as Force 17 had previously killed three United States ambassadors), then withdrew his approval. There was some loss of civilian life in the strike against the PLO; however, without Pollard's detailed information, the loss of civilians would certainly have been greater.

But the Pollard information on the military front probably had the greatest impact. Armed with new knowledge of Russian electronic systems, Israel sent a drone airplane over Damascus. The Syrians fired their missiles and they all missed, proving to Syrian President Assad that he lacked the military superiority with which he thought the Russians had supplied him.

Possibly that single act averted an almost certain outbreak of hostilities on the Golan Heights. Thus Arab lives were saved as well as Israeli, and the danger of American intervention was avoided.

In mid-1984, Jonathan Pollard was introduced to Aviem Sella, who was then taking graduate courses at New York University. He told Sella he knew certain information the United States was withholding which he felt was critical to Israel's survival. One can speculate that this initial information concerned the existence of the Syrian nerve-gas plants. Israel confirmed its importance, and then set up an organization in Israel and the United States to receive detailed information, analyze it rapidly, and direct the collection of additional information. In the United States, Israel science attaché, Yosef Yagur, became Pollard's "handler," responsible for collecting information. Copying equipment was set up at the apartment of Israeli embassy secretary Irit Erb, where Pollard would deliver the documents. Teams of military specialists and scientists met in Israel to make a quick analysis of the information and agree on requests for additional detailed information.

At Israel's Inner Cabinet level, decisions, such as the strike on Tunis and the sending of the drone plane over Damascus, were based on that information. In mid-1985, the Israeli government conveyed an official message of gratitude to Pollard.

Pollard's espionage activities for Israel lasted approximately thirteen months, a relatively short period as spy operations go. However, the pace of his activity was rapid and he succeeded in transferring over one hundred documents. During that time, he took two business trips to Europe, one of which included a stop in Israel, to meet with the Israeli officials. He took his fiancée, Anne Henderson, on both trips, and married her in Venice on the second trip, three months before his arrest. On both trips, Israeli officials brought their wives to "baby sit" Anne and to keep her away from the operations.

ANNE POLLARD'S STORY

When Anne Henderson met Jay (as he's known to friends) Pollard in 1981, the two became good friends almost immediately. Anne, then twenty-one, was working as a secretary in Washington, D.C., and attending college in the evening. She was struck not only by Jay's gentle manners and charm, but also by his intelligence, and the two shared many hours of good talk about national and world events. In addition, Jay offered Anne a deeper pride in and understanding of her Jewish heritage. Anne had been raised in a Jewish community in New Jersey and had participated in many Jewish religious and community activities there.

Shortly after they met, Anne was introduced to Jay's family, whom she grew to love and respect, as they did her. In 1982, Jay and Anne decided to share an apartment.

Although Jay discussed certain aspects of his work with Anne, she was deeply engrossed in her own career in public relations and did not really concern herself with his. By 1985 Anne was working for The National Rifle Association, where she was responsible for running the National Rifle Championships press office and for producing a variety of materials on U.S. Olympic teams and hunter and firearms safety.

In mid-1985 she was hired to direct the Washington office of a New York-based public-relations firm, to consult with established clients. She was to participate in profit sharing. Anne had a natural gift for writing and other communications, and had progressed rapidly in the field.

She was excited at the opportunity and began working night and day preparing new business presentations for potential clients and exploring new openings for the firm. Among the largest prospective accounts in Washington was the Chinese embassy. The Chinese understood little about America, particularly how to present themselves to the American public. For a public-relations firm, it was a potential gold mine. Jay's father, Dr. Morris Pollard, had met the Chinese ambassador and could offer a letter of introduction, so Anne's firm was allowed to make a presentation.

Part of the research normally done to prepare such presentations is collecting newspaper and magazine articles, a process which is speeded by their availability in computer information banks. Jay had access to these computer banks through a commercial program known as Nexis, and Anne asked him if he could bring her copies of these newspaper and magazine articles as part of her research.

Instead of the articles, Jay brought home directories of the Chinese embassy and several consular offices. These directories listed publically known departments and staffs, but also contained a few notations that were labeled secret, e.g., the names of people suspected of working for Chinese intelligence. Those directories, which Anne scanned rapidly, were of little value to her. In fact, she did not use any information from those directories since they were not related to the type of presentation she made. However one of her five-year prison sentences is based on the fact that she scanned the directories without authorization; that is, she did not possess security clearance. That was also the basis of her detention without bail and the labeling of her as a suspected Chinese communist spy by *The New York Times* and other publications. It was later to be the basis of the government's preventing her from talking directly to reporters.

Her firm made the presentation to the Chinese embassy in September 1985, over three months before her arrest. It did not result in any business and sometime later, another public relations firm, one of the nation's largest, obtained an important contract from the Chinese.

In the 1983–1984 period, Jay and Anne had often discussed some of his frustrations at work. Some of these concerned normal bureaucratic maneuvering by coworkers and supervisors. However, others were what Jay felt was a particularly strong anti-Semitic atmosphere, freely expressed in statements and jokes to Jay, since his coworkers did not know he was Jewish. Because this atmosphere was causing Jay anguish, Anne often suggested that he quit and take a job in a less stressful situation.

By 1984, Jay's unhappiness was increasing. Without giving Anne specific information, he let her know that things were happening that he believed would jeopardize Israel's existence. Anne continued to urge him to quit and suggested he seek employment with an Israeli-related lobbying or defense firm where he could more freely use his expertise to help Israel if that was what he desired.

But by late spring of 1984, Jay had met then-Colonel Sella in New York where he and his wife, Yudith, were taking graduate courses at New York University. Jay then made the fateful decision to provide Israel with the information he regarded as critical to its survival.

Later Jay introduced Sella and Yudith to Anne in Washington, where she was enchanted by their sophistication and charm. In the fall of 1984, Anne traveled to Paris with Jay, when he again met with Sella and other Israelis. While Jay met with them, their wives took Anne sightseeing around Paris. Later the Israelis sent Jay a ring to give to Anne as an engagement present from a fictional uncle—a cover story they had concocted to explain why he was making the trip. The ring, which Anne had valued at a Washington jeweler at $1,800, was later confiscated by the government as "loot."

When Anne discovered documents in the apartment labeled "secret," she confronted Jay and asked him not to bring them to their home. Jay swore to her that nothing he was doing involved United States defense secrets, but rather information about terrorist incidents and about hostile nations surrounding Israel. He convinced her that he was acting properly.

Nevertheless, her husband's work at Naval Intelligence Services bothered Anne, particularly because of the anti-Semitic attitudes there. By the following spring, 1985, however, she was engrossed in her new job and too busy to worry. She was aware that what he was doing was probably illegal, but she agreed with his moral stance.

Was Anne legally—if not ethically—bound to report Jay to the authorities? She has said that such a thought never even crossed her mind. She loved Jay deeply and believed that his actions were justified. In fact, in Anne's mind, Jay was a hero because he was acting to preserve America's ally, Israel, without in any way jeopardizing the security of the United States. She believed he was, in effect, saving lives. In any event, she was never charged with any crime relating to failure to turn Jay in.

In the summer of 1985, Anne and Jay decided to get married. Intitially, the ceremony was to take place in Washington; however, Jay's Israeli team had told him to take a trip to Israel and Europe in order to confer with them, and to bring his fiancée. Anne and Jay used the opportunity to wed in Venice in August.

By November 1985, Anne had finished the first part of her training and was scheduled to begin the advanced section, starting work on Monday, November 25. A week earlier, however, her world collapsed.

On Sunday, November 17, Jay was scheduled to pick up documents at the apartment of Irit Erb, the Israeli embassy secretary who did the copying. Erb failed to answer the doorbell, and Jay became concerned that something was happening. (It later turned out that she was unavailable for personal reasons.) Jay began to worry that he might be in trouble, and later that day, he made a pact with Anne: If he should ever telephone her and use the code word "cactus," she was to get rid of any documents that happened to be in the apartment. He chose "cactus" because he had some cactus plants in their living room.

THE ARRESTS

On Monday, November 18, Jay and Anne were scheduled to have dinner at a restaurant with Aviem Sella and his wife, who were visiting in Washington that day—a social occasion. At 5:00 P.M., as was his custom, Jay phoned Anne to say he was leaving work and would be home by 5:30. Their date with the Sellas was not until 8:00.

When Jay failed to arrive by 6:00, Anne called his office and was told that he had been seen leaving the building an hour earlier. She grew alarmed, believing he might have car trouble, or been involved in an accident. By 7:30 she was frantic. Something terrible must have happened. But shortly after, he did call. "I'm still at the office," he said, which Anne knew to be untrue, "but can you meet our friends at the restaurant and bring them the cactus." He phoned her again and repeated the message.

In a panic, Anne hastily rounded up his papers. She stuffed them into a suitcase that already contained a few of her personal belongings, and slipped out of the apartment. She raced down the stairwell, lugging the heavy suitcase, and turned toward the back area of the apartment building. Through the door, she caught a glimpse of a number of strange cars in which were seated somber-looking men, unknown to her. Shoving the suitcase under the stairs, she returned to her own floor and went to the neighbors, the Esfandiaris.

"Look," she asked Babak, who answered the door, "I left a suitcase downstairs. Would you take it to the Four Seasons Hotel for me? It's too heavy for me to carry. I'll meet you there."

Babak stared at her. "Anne is something wrong?"

She told him that Jay hadn't shown up yet and she was terribly worried about him, but he continued to hesitate. Finally she explained that the suitcase contained some papers of Jay's and she didn't want anyone to find them in the apartment.

In the end, the neighbor did lug the suitcase to the hotel but he failed to spot Anne there, and returned to his apartment with it. Later he called the FBI.

For that abortive attempt to help her husband, Anne Pollard received another five-year prison sentence, the technical charge being "accessory after the fact to possession of national security documents."

Later that evening, Anne called Sella at his hotel and met him at another restaurant. She apologized for failing to show up for dinner, and told him she thought Jay was in serious trouble. Sella gave her the phone number in New York of Yosef Yagur, Jay's "handler," and told her to call him, but first to wait for several hours. When Anne returned to her apartment, she found Jay there, with dozens of federal agents at work tearing the apartment apart in their search for classified documents. It was 2:00 A.M. before the agents left, and Jay was able to explain what had happened. They had stopped him outside the building where he worked and searched his briefcase, which contained classified documents. They had spent several hours interrogating him about his possession of this material, but they apparently did not have enough evidence to make an arrest, because Jay had standing permission to remove documents he was working on from his work place.

Later that day, Tuesday, November 19, federal agents resumed their questioning of Jay and again on Wednesday the twentieth. That evening Jay called the Israeli embassy, requesting sanctuary, and asked Anne if she would go to Israel with him. Anne told him she would, an act which would violate no law. The Israelis told Jay simply to arrive there at 10 A.M. and he would be escorted to Israel.

On Thursday, November 21, Jay drove Anne to her doctor for a scheduled operation to break up a cellular mass in her stomach by inserting an instrument down her throat. While she was still groggy from the sedative, he drove to the Israeli embassy—losing his way briefly in traffic because Jay was unsure of the building's exact location—and through the open gates into the front yard. Initially they were greeted warmly by waiting security guards, who said, "You are home. Do not worry." One of the guards went inside the building. When he returned a few minutes later, he ordered Jay and Anne off the premises.

American agents, waiting outside the grounds, immediately arrested Jay.

Because Anne was still under sedation, the agents accompanied her back to her apartment and waited until she recovered. Then they confiscated her purse, which contained her medications and prescriptions, as well as her personal identification, credit cards, money, and so on and left. The following day, after she visited her husband in the D.C. jail, Anne was arrested. She spent the next ninety-five days in isolated detention.

THE ISSUES

The Israel government took a stand in the Pollard case by furnishing evidence and testimony necessary to convict him and by denying it had any official knowledge that the espionage was occurring. It has been widely reported that the American government was of two minds about how to handle the case. The intelligence community and the State Department wanted the matter handled quietly, as virtually all previous cases of friendly nation spying had been handled, because of the possible political sensitivities. The Justice Department and the Defense Department, however, pressed for maximum prosecution and maximum sentences. In the end, Justice and Defense prevailed.

The case presented legal, moral and political issues. Legally Jonathan Pollard had broken a law that provides for a sentence from one year to life imprisonment. People who have violated that law in the past have had the charges dropped and been quietly expelled, if they were foreign nationals, or have received relatively light sentences. In one 1986 case shortly preceding the Pollard pleading, Sharon Scranage was convicted of spying for Ghana and received a five-year sentence, which was later reduced to two years. In 1985 Samuel Loring Morison, a naval employee who sold classified information to an English publication, received two years. Earlier in 1982, Ensign Stephen Baba was sentenced to eight years for selling secret documents to South Africa, a sentence which was reduced in plea bargaining to only two years.

Looking at classified documents without authorization is a crime with which many reporters or countless other people could be charged. Now, after Anne Pollard's precedent-setting successful conviction, government prosecutors have an open road to pursue arrest, detention without bail, and conviction of any number of these people.

The prosecution of Anne Pollard was highly selective, to say the least. For example, the wife of a man recently prosecuted for spying for the Soviet Union was not even charged with a crime, despite the fact that she not only knew of her husband's activities for eighteen years, but also participated in delivering documents and collecting money. Ironically, the wife of another Russian spy and ex-CIA agent successfully arranged her husband's escape to Russia at the very time Anne was cooperating with the American government through her plea-bargaining agreement. The woman was never charged with any crime.

The moral issues involved are more complex. Certainly, from Jonathan Pollard's point of view, his actions were necessary to preserve Israel as well as to save lives. In Pollard's case, there was no provable damage to United States security, other than speculative issues, and no compromising of agents. Probably the most compelling moral issue is that the punishments did not fit the crime, and one needs to look elsewhere to determine the reasons they were so severe.

The political issues involved are controversial. Defense Secretary Caspar Weinberger argued that Pollard upset his plan for a balance of power in the Middle East by making Israel too strong. Many people in government, however, believe that a strong Israel is America's best assurance of peace in the Middle East, as well as defense against Soviet expansion. Perhaps time will tell.

Underlying Weinberger's directions to the court is a very serious issue as to whether the head of the military in the United States ought to be involved in foreign policy, a role traditionally reserved to Congress, the President, and the Secretary of State under Constitutional authority.

Opinion is also divided on whether or not Anne Pollard should have received a five-year sentence. Some argue that since she not only knew what her husband was doing and failed to turn him in to the authorities, but cooperated with him at the last minute in attempting to remove the documents from their apartment, she should also be punished. Others say that her punishment was simply a prosecutorial tool to elicit full cooperation from Jay. Whether that is true or not, it certainly produced that effect. Much of his cooperation was based on his belief that he was helping Anne.

THE PROSECUTION

The prosecutors made extensive use of the press in presenting their case, a technique that is prohibited in many nations, like Great Britain, because of its possible unfair effect on the public, and subsequently juries and judges.

At first, the government issued a press release explaining that Anne had been arrested because it was thought she "might have" given the Chinese communists American secrets. This made front-page news even for such normally unsensational newspapers as *The New York Times*. That was bad enough, but the *Times* and other publications continued to report that Anne was an accessory to her husband's espionage.

In the Pollard case, the prosecutors' tactics were also designed to head off possible public sympathy for the defense. Lead prosecutor Joseph Di Genova bragged to Jonathan Pollard that he would make it impossible for any Jew in America, let alone anyone else, to support him. To the press and court, Di Genova created fictional Pollards: evil mercenaries motivated by high living and greed. Stories were leaked to reporters that the Pollards used drugs and quoted fictional "friends" or "sources" saying Jonathan Pollard had mental problems and was unstable. The charges made the newspapers but their unsensational denial was not newsworthy.

These tactics of Di Genova's were successful. No support was forthcoming for the defense until over a year after the arrests.

Ultimately however, the Pollard's sentences were determined by politics. A message from Secretary of Defense Caspar Weinberger to the officiating judge, Aubrey E. Robinson, Jr.—delivered by courier, for effect on March 3, 1987, one day before the public sentencing hearing—demanded that the punishment send a political message to Israel: America's national honor had been insulted. According to a published letter from Jonathan Pollard cleared by Naval Intelligence, Weinberger, reportedly a Christian convert from Judaism, said the promotion of Colonel Sella to general and commander of the Tel Nof Air Base should be "visited upon the defendants' heads." Judge Robinson gave maximum sentences to both Pollards.

Weinberger was also reported to have stated that both Jay and Anne "had succumbed to the same virus of treason which had infected the Rosenbergs." This is a strange remark, considering that Jay was never charged with treason.

THE PLEA BARGAINS

Both Jonathan and Anne Pollard had earlier reached an agreement with federal prosecutors, signed in June 1986, which called for them to plead guilty to the separate charges and to cooperate fully in a lengthy investigation of the two separate cases. In return

for the pleas and for the cooperation, they were to be given leniency.

The separate plea-bargain agreements were contingent on each
other—in other words, the government refused to make one valid
without the other. Anne was told that unless she signed her agreement, the government would insist on a life sentence for Jay, but if
she signed, he would receive leniency. Jay was told that unless he
signed, the government would not only add charges against him
but would also prosecute his wife harshly. If he signed, they would
go easy on her. In addition, both Pollards were threatened with
further physical punishment of Anne by withholding her medication, as had been done during her detention.

The ink on the agreement was not dry before the government
began reneging. The first indication was the scheduling of the
plea-agreement date to coincide with the Congressional debate on
the sale of arms to Saudi Arabia. With headlines screaming "Israeli
Spies Plead Guilty!" Congress narrowly approved the arms sale.

The second indication was the government's increased efforts to
tie prominent Jews in the government to the spying. Jay was given
a list of names and told he could expect further leniency if he would
just implicate one or more of them. Jay refused.

In addition to these pressures, Jay was continually in solitary
confinement.

Anne had expected that, once the government fully understood
all the details about the affair, it would admit its mistake about
spying for the Chinese and other stories printed about her. Instead,
the prosecution kept concocting new stories to replace the ones
proved false. A witness appeared who testified, in secret, that Anne
tried to recruit him. Anne's polygraph interpreted otherwise. The
government refused to allow the secret witness to be polygraphed
or even cross-examined. Obviously, the prosecutors knew the story
was false, but intended to bring it before the judge and to publicize
it anyway.

THE ATTEMPT TO BE HEARD

Finally Anne Pollard fully understood that the government had
no intention of honoring its agreement. Her year-long silence had
only resulted in the prosecutors being able to portray her and her
husband falsely, and that their cooperation, instead of earning

them leniency, was being used against them. She began to realize that she might wind up behind bars, silenced, with no chance to tell her side of the story or to lobby for her husband's release.

To insure that the silence would not be total, Anne and Jonathan Pollard agreed to be interviewed by one journalist and selected Wolf Blitzer, Washington correspondent for *The Jerusalem Post*. Blitzer, a native of Buffalo, New York, was widely respected for his knowledge of United States-Israeli relations and had a great many information sources in both nations.

Blitzer interviewed Jay and Anne Pollard and then checked their information with his own informants. The Pollards restricted the interviews solely to discussions about unclassified information. In addition to reporting Jay Pollard's motivations, Blitzer uncovered, from high-level sources in the United States and Israel, several specific examples of information Jay had provided. His reports allowed Israelis to understand, for the first time, something of the significance of what had happened and that the information had been provided by someone with deep Zionist convictions and sense of moral obligations. Blitzer's articles also began appearing in Jewish publications in the United States.

The prosecutors reacted to this view of the case by threatening both Jay and Anne with additional punishment if anything further were said. In addition, Jay was subjected to a series of punishments in prison. In December 1986, for example, on the Jewish holiday of Hanukkah, a guard told him he was "going home to Israel." Instead he was chained by his arms, legs, and neck, and was spreadeagled to both sides of an unheated van. In this painful position, he was driven, in icy weather at nearly 100 miles per hour, from Petersburg, Virginia, to the federal prison in Lewisburg, Pennsylvania, where he was placed in a cell without either blanket or mattress. Of course, that also made it impossible for any reporter to contact him.

Anne realized that her freedom might also be jeopardized, but she reacted by making sure her story would be told if she were incarcerated.

She agreed to be interviewed by Mike Wallace on 60 *Minutes,* provided he would not broadcast the interview until after March 4, the sentencing date. Wallace and 60 *Minutes* agreed, but promptly broke that agreement once they had several hours of interview with her on tape. Wallace has also attempted to interview Jay for this program, but was denied permission by the United States government.

The edited tape was broadcast on March 1 in such a way that it appeared that Anne had been part of the espionage operation. Her remarks had been edited to indicate that she was aware of her husband's activities and supported them. Anne herself did not come across well in the interview, partially because of her physical pain, lack of sleep and stress. Many of her close friends were shocked at what they perceived as a "butcher job" on the part of Wallace. But Anne had accomplished her major goal by obtaining a public airing of Jay's position.

Anne hoped principally to discredit the government's claim that Jay and she were mercenaries, motivated only by greed. For over a year, government propagandists had fed that story to the press. In her interview, Anne was partially successful in countering it, since press reports began to describe Pollard's Zionist convictions as his primary motivation.

Before she was totally silenced on March 4, Anne Pollard took one other step. She taped a long interview for Israeli TV, which was broadcast in Israel on March 4. More extensive than *60 Minutes* and more carefully edited, the interview electrified the Israelis. When they learned of the harsh sentences imposed that day, along with the Caspar Weinberger statement that it was a "message to Israel," the Israeli people reacted strongly.

At the government level, the shaky coalition government narrowly survived four no-confidence votes and eventually agreed to a limited inquiry. The reaction against the government was not a plea by the public to punish associates of Pollard, as was widely reported in the American press, but rather to ask why the government failed to support Pollard. On the streets, Citizens for the Pollards committees were formed, and for the first time, funds were collected to help pay the huge legal bills they and their families had amassed up to that point.

Although both Pollards are now prohibited from talking to any reporter, and consequently to the public, except through written questions and answers censored by the government, the brief statements they have already made and those included in this book do much to explain what happened and why.

In addition, Jay was successful in getting out of prison a long letter, dated June 29, 1987, addressed to Robert Cohn, the editor of the *St. Louis Jewish Light*, which is included in this book, starting on page 184. Its detailed explanation of his actions and their deliberate misinterpretation and distortion by the government make one wonder what has happened to the concept of justice as we traditionally associate it with American democracy.

JONATHAN JAY POLLARD
A SHORT BIOGRAPHY

At 4:22 A.M. on Saturday, August 7, 1954, Mildred Pollard gave birth to the youngest of her three children. Jonathan Jay Pollard was helped into the world by doctors from the University of Texas Medical Branch in Galveston, largely because his father, Dr. Morris Pollard, was a professor there. His older brother, Harvey, was later to become a doctor while his sister, Carol, was to become a symphony musician.

Dr. Pollard was already a microbiologist of some renown. He had received four Presidential citations for his work on antibodies during World War II for his willingness to use his own body for tests rather than to wait for more orthodox time-consuming procedures.

Members of Mildred Pollard's family were also in the medical profession. Her brother was commander of the U.S. Army Hospital in Paris at the end of World War II.

Jonathan Pollard was born with the advantages his parents could bestow, both genetically and socially. Genetically, he was possessed with a powerful intellect and a talent for music, if also a somewhat smallish physical body. Socially, he had the advantages of a secure middle-class family.

However the general atmosphere for young children in Texas does not really favor young boys interested in books and music, particularly if they are small and quiet—and Jewish. Jay was the type of youngster class bullies found it easy to pick on. He often came home bloodied and beaten, much to the dismay of his mother.

Dr. Pollard was later to join the University of Notre Dame and eventually to head one of its most prestigious departments, the Lobund Laboratory. He was also to travel extensively and to lecture and teach at various universities around the world.

When the Pollards moved to South Bend, Indiana, when Jonathan was nine, the boy hoped to escape the harshness of the Texas environment. Instead, the neighborhood where the family settled was on the outskirts of a blue-collar community in a deep economic recession. It was easy to blame hard times on others, especially Jews. In defense, Jonathan retreated into a world centered around his Hebrew school, where he could feel at home with other Jewish children and where he could concentrate on the books and the music he loved. He became a first-rate cello player and was always near the top of his class academically.

The Pollards were a deeply religious family, fully cognizant of its Jewish roots, and ardent supporters of Israel. His mother's brother not only donated medical supplies to the new Israeli army, but also managed to secure surplus U.S. Army boots for it.

Although Dr. Pollard himself was born on a farm in New York State, his parents had emigrated from Lithuania. After World War II, when he attempted to contact his relatives there, he learned that all seventy-five who had remained in Europe had perished in the Holocaust. When Jonathan was in his early teens, his father took him to visit those extermination camps where their kin had been murdered.

These personal experiences left an indelible impression on young Jonathan. To him, "Never again" became more than mere words. Back in South Bend, he found many of his Jewish schoolmates expressing similar views. although perhaps not as strongly. In fact, roughly half of his schoolmates later emigrated to Israel.

As an undergraduate at Stanford, Jay was a brilliant student. He was a voracious reader and he went far beyond required texts. His tastes included history and philosophy, as well as foreign affairs and government. He studied languages, supplementing his fluency in Hebrew with fluency in German, and some acquaintanceship with other European languages, Arabic, and Africaans. His graduate courses at Fletcher continued in the same vein, while emphasizing military strategies. Although he completed enough courses to receive his Masters Degree in international affairs, he received a job offer in a United States intelligence service before making his degree application, and hurried to Washington.

Jay found the intelligence services a place to enlarge his knowledge, while providing him the opportunity to use that which he already possessed. His superiors in naval intelligence often turned to the young civilian to prepare analyses on complex subjects, rather than to his much older and more experienced coworkers. They also gave him operational assignments, something virtually rarely done for an analyst in the intelligence services. They awarded him two letters of commendation and a special citation from the Secretary of the Navy.

ANNE HENDERSON POLLARD
A SHORT BIOGRAPHY

Anne Louise Henderson was a beautiful person from the day she was born on May 1, 1960—not just in appearance, but also in temperament. The first few days after her birth, with other babies crying around her, little Anne was the picture of peace and contentment, a disposition she maintained throughout her life to the time of her imprisonment. Her grandfather, Nathanial Topper, who was close to her throughout his life, delighted staring at her for hours in the hospital nursery and relatives of other newborns invariably stopped to look at the beautiful red-headed baby.

After her mother brought her home and took her shopping at a local Brooklyn supermarket, a woman, who had been staring at her admiringly, gave a startled yelp. "The doll moved!" she exclaimed.

Anne was almost born in Chile. In 1959, her father, Bernard R. Henderson, was a mine foreman at the huge Chuquicamata, Chile, copper mine, then owned by Anaconda Company. But when his wife, Elaine, became pregnant with Anne, they thought that the 10,000-foot altitude at Chuquicamata would make the birth difficult, so the Hendersons returned to New York where Bernard became an editor for *Engineering & Mining Journal*.

Anne's mother is a native New Yorker; most of her family are conservative or orthodox Jews. Anne was brought up to share the many Jewish traditions and holidays with her mother's relatives, the Lessersons, Auslanders, and Toppers.

Anne enjoyed a close family life. Her parents took her to almost every social function they attended: visits to her Jewish aunts, uncles and cousins, holiday celebrations, birthdays, outings, and school events.

The Hendersons took many weekend trips and family vacations. Some weekends, they traveled to Canada or upstate New York, often camping out. In that way, Anne was able to visit such places as Nova Scotia, Mexico, and several Caribbean islands, in addition to meeting her father's relatives in Montana, Idaho, Washington, and California.

Anne was always an asset on trips. In Mexico, for example, her red hair was considered lucky by the Mexican people, who used to line up to touch her for good fortune. In French Canada, her French fluency won the family many friends and the best of service in restaurants. At the Copacabana nightclub celebrating her grandfather's birthday, Sergio Franchi changed his act to do a Romeo and Juliet duet with Anne.

When Anne was two years old, the family moved to a predominantly Jewish community in White Meadow Lake, New Jersey, a Morris County suburb with a large synagogue, a clubhouse, three beaches, and many recreational facilities. Anne made many friends and became active in Jewish youth groups as well as other social organizations. At school, she was a model student with outstanding grades. Her singing voice was good enough to win her parts in many community plays and other presentations.

Anne was six when her brother John was born; partly because Anne was much older, no sibling rivalry ever developed. Instead, Anne became a combination of sister, friend, and mother to her young brother. In all the years the two youngsters were growing up, the Hendersons never had to hire a babysitter.

When Anne was in the sixth grade, she was selected as a teaching assistant for the kindergarten class. That resulted in many babysitting jobs, which gave her extra spending money and a sense of independence.

While Anne was growing up in New Jersey, her father worked at various editing jobs in the New York area. When she was fifteen, he was named head of public relations for a division of Gulf & Western, and later press secretary of the Teamsters Union. When she was eighteen, Anne went to live with her father in Washington, D.C., finished high school, began college, and also began working at her own career in public relations.

Some stress was put on Anne in her teen-age years because of the breakup of her parents' marriage and their divorce in 1979. That change in her environment, coupled with her natural mothering of her younger brother, tended to give Anne a maturity beyond her years as well as an inner drive to work hard and succeed at any task.

When her father left Washington in 1980, Anne stayed on to work in the nation's capital and became fully independent. Her first job was as secretary to a chemical association, but she soon asked for and was given extra responsibility arranging their various meetings. In addition to taking courses in journalism and public relations at the University of Maryland at night, Anne used her employment environment to learn as many skills as possible. By the time she met Jay Pollard in 1981, she had already established herself as a competent writer and public-relations professional.

Anne and Jay were good friends from the time they met. She was attracted to Jay's intellect but equally important, to his commitment to Judaism and Zionism. She liked his tender and almost fatherly qualities and also saw in him a way of being proud to be Jewish. They became a couple who discussed issues in a close and understanding way, and were very loving to each other.

Her grandfather, Nathanial Topper, to whom she had been very close all her life, died in December, 1986, at the age of ninety-six, in Miami Beach, Florida. From his hospital bed, he asked to see Anne "one last time," unaware of the charges against her. Anne received permission from the government to visit him, and he died peacefully one hour after seeing his beloved granddaughter.

LETTER TO SENTENCING JUDGE FROM BERNARD HENDERSON ON BEHALF OF JONATHAN JAY POLLARD

Falls Church, VA 22041
Feb. 2, 1987

Chief Judge Aubrey E.
   Robinson, Jr.
United States District Court for
the District of Columbia
Washington, D.C. 20001

Dear Chief Judge Robinson:

If ever a person had a right to harshly judge someone for a perceived personal injury, it is I as the father in law of Jonathan Jay Pollard. By falling in love with him, and marrying him, and standing by him, my daughter endangered her life and was tragically punished.

How much easier her life would be had she simply walked away from him. Yet there are compelling reasons why she did not.

Jay Pollard is a gentle person in the full sense of the word—kind, caring and considerate. He is also a deep intellectual, and provided Anne with the kind of care and companionship that allowed her much happiness.

If he had a fault, it was idealism; believing as young people often do that they should contribute to improving society: In his case, protecting his Jewish heritage as well as protecting U.S. citizens from terrorists and military threats.

I am an American whose ancestors were shipped here during the notorious clearances of the Scottish highlands. While I continue to hold a special concern for my Scottish relatives, like other Americans I understand the special concerns of people of different ancestry. I understand and can empathize with the passionate desire of Jews to avoid future Holocausts through the maintenance of their ancestral homeland. And I understand the special courage it takes to act for the preservation of one's ideals, particularly when those ideals cause deep emotional and legal conflicts.

Because Jay Pollard is imbued with high moral standards, he was able to contribute to the preservation of his racial homeland without jeopardizing the security of his national homeland. In fact, I subscribe to the argument that he has strengthened U.S. defenses in so doing, and much more importantly has helped avert an Arab-Israeli war into which American soldiers would likely have been drawn.

I have been deeply distressed throughout his long year and half of isolated detention that the U.S. attorneys in this case have chosen to make the case a political one rather than a legal one. In choosing the political route for prosecution, they have concocted stories, mostly for the benefit of the press and public opinion, steeped in character assassination and racial bigotry.

As a public relations professional, I witnessed a prosecutorial public relations machine in action using every trick of the trade: a barrage of controlled leaks with unattributed sources; prerelease of court documents to the press at press deadline times so as to prevent reply; timing of releases to coincide with Congressional debates related to the case (the approval of arms for Saudi Arabia); etc.

By their actions, the prosecutors have determined that the political aspects of this case far outweigh any factual or legal aspects. Perhaps they are right; but if in so doing they are allowed to cause more than just punishment to be inflicted on this ethical human being, their mountain of lies will receive undeserved credibility for the moment.

This is an historical case with enormous racial and political overtones which will be dissected and examined piece by piece for years and decades to come—not only by people in the United States, but also by people in many other countries.

I pray that your judgement is tempered by facts and mercy, and that Jonathan Jay Pollard be allowed to resume a productive role in society as soon as possible. I pray that he may rejoin his wife, my daughter, as quickly as possible so that they may continue to share the special love they have for each other in the spirit of life, liberty and the pursuit of happiness to which they have been so long denied.

Very sincerely yours,

Bernard R. Henderson

ANNE POLLARD'S LETTER TO ATTORNEY
LEON CHARNEY

Falls Church, VA 22041
February 10, 1987

Leon H. Charney
One State Street Plaza
New York, N.Y. 10004

Dear Mr. Charney,

Thank you very much for, at the request of myself, my husband Jonathan Jay Pollard, and my father, Bernard Henderson, accepting our appeal that you become lead attorney in our case and for speaking to the press on our behalf. We all had made a firm decision that you were to be the primary spokesman for our case.

While we subsequently agreed to the Hibeys' press release describing themselves as the sole spokespersons for the criminal charges pending against us, this was based on information disclosed to my husband on the evening of January 8, while I was not apprised of it until later the following day, well after your greatly appreciated efforts. I asked my father to inform you of this unanticipated development the moment I learned of it. We are still evaluating both the accuracy of the information and its importance, realizing that it may have been overstated, possibly grossly.

I humbly request that you continue for the time being to act as a political adviser to my husband and I [sic], and that you consider reentering the legal case at a future time in whatever role we mutually feel would be warranted.

Aside from the new information, we have also been advised that leniency at sentencing may be shown to us provided we don't renounce our American citizenship in court. The reason is that that leniency would, in itself, facilitate any subsequent political resolution; while harsh sentences could create a more difficult political resolution. While this rationale is speculative, it does contain some logic, particularly because the possibility exists that the non-espionage, catch-all charges to which I have plead [sic] guilty, do not necessarily warrant further incarceration. In that event, I would be better able to help my husband. Additionally, our judicial fates are tied to one another. If I received a minimal sentence or probation, the judge would be less inclined to give my husband a life sentence.

That is not to say this decision was motivated by the possibility that I would escape a harsh prison sentence or even a prison sentence at the expense of my husband. Nor does it mean that Jay will necessarily receive a lenient sentence. I am a devoted wife and am deeply in love with my husband. I live with the daily anxiety and torment of a possible lengthy separation from Jay and I will spare no effort to assure his best possible future. However, you must realize that extraordinary pressures have been put on us. These are caused by the anxiety and uncertainty of our future; our tortuous separation; the horrendous isolated living conditions I was subjected to while incarcerated and that Jay has been continually subjected to for over a year; and the intense pressures placed on us by the prosecutors, law enforcement officials and news media.

In the wake of Wolf Blitzer's superb articles and the tremendous efforts of an American physician, Dr. Julian Ungar-Sargon, to have my husband's letter to him published worldwide, we believe the government has become very fearful that the true facts and motivations relating to our alleged "criminal activities" will at long last be known by the public. Recently we were threatened by the Justice Department with additional penalties for our interviews with Wolf Blitzer, and advised that any additional form of communication by us to anyone ranging from family to religious leaders to the press will result in very serious unspecified consequences. The government is literally interpreting our plea agreement to mean that we can never discuss any aspect of our lives or of the case with anyone. While our plea agreement states that we may not disclose classified information to the time of sentencing, we have never, nor would ever, disclose classified information to the press or public at any time. While we would never harm the United States or Israel by doing so, I cannot say the same for the prosecutors.

Since our arrest a torrent of disinformation has been fed to the press in which unidentified government officials have revealed specific classified information about our case. As one example, *The Washington Post* reported on June 5, 1986, "The classified information the Israelis received included technical assessments of radar and other electronic equipment used by Egypt, Saudi Arabia and possibly Jordan to monitor Middle East activities." Nearly a week before the fact, the press was reporting we intended to plead guilty through a plea bargain agreement and that a prominent Israeli Air Force Colonel may be indicted. The prosecutors went so far as to name specific classified documents in the government's factual proffer about me dated June 4, 1986.

The prosecutors allege that my husband's activities severely impacted American-Arab relations. However it was the prosecutors who caused the major damage by turning our hearings and pleading sessions into major media events. Had this affair been handled quietly, there would have been no damage to those relations. However the U.S. Attorneys in Washington continually orchestrated a series of controlled leaks about our case designed to embarrass Israel, the American Jewish community and Zionists. Members of the press have described these leaks and sources to me. *The Washington Post* on June 7, 1986, put it in writing: "One senior official singled out U.S. Attorney Joseph E. di Genova as a source of the leaks detailing the extent of the Israeli operation, saying "di Genova wants to stick it to Israel. He opposed the (Pollard) plea bargaining from the very beginning because he wanted to cash in on the publicity that a sensational trial would bring him. Now he is trying to make the case bigger than it is. He's enjoying the limelight . . . Who knows? Maybe it will get him elected to the Senate!"

I believe di Genova is mainly responsible for the grotesque slander about our purported lifestyle and motivation. He keeps leaking additional stories to the press about indicting my husband's alleged Israeli co-conspirators in an effort to indicate Israeli spying is rampant in the United States so as to damage Israeli-American relationships. He is well known among the Washington press corps as a man who thrives on personal recognition through publicity in the belief it will further his political ambitions. In this case, he has put his political beliefs and aspirations ahead of the national interest.

If anyone should be subject to a "gag order," it should be di Genova and other prosecutors who continue to disclose classified information and continue to concoct stories which damage our relationships not only with Israel, but also with "friendly Arab nations."

However, the prosecutors continue their incessant campaign of character assassination of us, attempting to portray us as, in their own words, "mercenaries driven by need and greed." The money was never a motivating force for my husband's actions. We are outraged that we have been forcibly silenced by the government from revealing the truth concerning our lifestyle; motivation; political, racial and ideological convictions; and moreover, our passionate concern for the preservation of American and Israeli lives. We are disheartened that no one, particularly in the Jewish community (with the exception of Wolf Blitzer, my father, Dr. Ungar-Sargon and yourself), has come to our defense publicly to correct the prosecutor's blatantly malicious and blasphemous allegations about us and their gross mischaracterization of the facts.

Although the prosecutors have deliberately set out to poison the air with their unmitigated fiction to create a horrendous portrait of us, we have nonetheless, received numerous private letters and expressions of support. These individuals have expressed their absolute outrage and incomprehension of the prosecutors' sadistic handling of our case.

We desperately seek to "liberate" the truth pertaining to our convictions and moral obligations as both loyal Americans and ardent Zionists. Jay and I will not continue to tolerate this allegedly enforceable "gag order." We intend to vigorously challenge the government's blatant attempt to strip us of our Constitutional First Amendment rights and are prepared to fight for our rights through the legal system as far as the Supreme Court if necessary.

My husband never engaged in any activities directed against the United States. In fact, he indirectly strengthened the United States by strengthening our most vital, most strategically important, and most dependable friend, Israel. Jay is a hero in the true sense of the word because he has ultimately preserved human life through averting a potential Arab-Israeli war by providing Israel with information critical to its continued existence.

Jay accomplished his main objectives in undertaking this operation: He has helped make Israel militarily superior to its enemies, and his contributions have had a profound impact on Israel's battle against state-sponsored and isolated terrorism. God knows that overt acts of brutal terrorist incidents, such as the barbaric slaughter of Israeli victims in Larnaca and the savage murder of Leon Klinghoffer during the hijacking of the cruise ship, the *Achille Lauro,* greatly upset us. The needless bombing of the Marine compound in Beirut in 1983 incenses us. Furthermore, the U.S. intelligence community's endemic, vicious anti-Semitic senti- ments, reactions and their deliberate withholding of critical infor- mation despite their knowledge of impending terrorist incidents against Jews world-wide infuriated us. Jay would often come across intelligence information crucial to the survival of Israel and when he inquired as to why the U.S. was not forthcoming with this data, his superiors would reply, "Oh let the Jews lose some planes and lives and they'll eventually figure out what they should have done to have prevented these incidents."

As Diaspora Jews, our families instilled in us the vital importance of preserving human life through the deterrence of war. Their convictions stemmed largely from their recent memory of World War II, in which 6,000,000 Jews were systematically massacred during the Holocaust. As a result of our upbringing, our perceived moral and racial obligations dictate that we should do everything in our power to prevent another systematic slaughter of mankind (especially Jews) from ever occurring again whether it is directed against a nation or a person. Human life is too precious to sacrifice. It is because of this rationale that Jay and I felt compelled to take certain actions which have ultimately resulted in our own personal Holocaust.

It was when Jay learned that a new generation of ultra sophisti- cated military equipment was being quietly positioned into the arsenals by our most despised enemies that he realized he could not stand idly by and witness the potential destruction of our racial homeland. Because of his dismay over these developments, Jay knew he could not close his eyes to this discovery for his family would have been sacrificed in vain during the Holocaust. He un- derstood that it was his racial obligation to apprise Israeli officials of these developments, and it was with this discovery that Jay began his dedicated service to the Israeli people.

Jay's Israeli "handler" regularly apprised him of how critically vital and valuable the information was that he provided to them by detailing the Israeli's ultimate use of it.

My only crime was that of being a loyal and devoted wife and ardent supporter of Israel. I am often asked that if I could recreate the events of November 18, 1985, knowing what I do today, would I again attempt to help my husband in his hour of need? Would I ultimately sacrifice my life to save the lives of essential Israeli officials and their respective spouses, including one General who is known for his heroic exploits and is considered to be a future leader of the State? The answer to both questions is an emphatic yes.

I am continually dumbfounded and appalled when people suggest to me that I could have avoided prosecution if I had turned my husband in to the authorities before my arrest and/or condemned his actions after my arrest. These abominable suggestions never presented themselves as alternatives because I would never do anything to hurt my husband or Israel. I am deeply in love with Jay and am vehemently supportive of Israel.

How the prosecutors can attempt to paint our convictions and actions to be those of greedy mercenaries is both contemptible and as diametrically opposite as night and day. Their recent endeavor to concoct stories that I allegedly recruited a "friend" for the espionage operation is as baseless and absurd as their original tale that I was a Chinese communist spy. Apart from being transparently obviously illogical since I have never participated in any espionage activity on behalf of anyone, this character's assertions are clearly a desperate attempt to trade my life for his, and the prosecutors have decided to overlook his perjury in an effort to build a case against me.

Indeed, the prosecution has deliberately overlooked some crucial points about our case, particularly Jay's single-handed efforts to save human lives and to deter overt acts of terrorism. I ask:

(1) If the United States now routinely exchanges classified information of the same magnitude as those documents my husband initially provided to Israeli officials, as has been reported, why is my husband being prosecuted?

(2) Unlike the recent spate of Russian spies who committed treason against the United States and severely damaged the national security, my husband only provided data pertaining to eminent Arab threats to Israel, and therefore did not damage U.S. national security because no U.S. classified defense information was compromised. Since Israel and the United States are allies and share many common enemies, and Israel takes care of the "dirty work" on behalf of the U.S. because the U.S. bureaucracy is unable to carry it out, why is my husband being prosecuted?

(3) As the United States and Israel have waged a war against state-

sponsored and isolated terrorism, both nations see eye-to-eye on the culpability of the players. Both nations have participated actively in deterring terrorism through force: i.e., Israel raided PLO leader Yasser Arafat's Force 17 in Tunis while the U.S. bombed Tripoli and Benghasi. Recently the U.S. has been persistently victimized by these demented, fanatical groups sponsored by Syria, Iran and Libya. Some examples which come to mind range from the relentless kidnapping of Americans and the bombing of the Marine compound in Beirut to the massacre of passengers at the Rome and Vienna airports. While not victimized as often as the U.S. (because of their well known and appreciated ability to fend off terrorism), Israel has forever assisted in each one of its crisis. Again I ask, why is my husband being prosecuted?

(4) It was reported that Syrian President Assad has incessantly discussed the potential of war between Syria and Israel because:

—He does not wish to be known in history as the man who lost the Golan Heights which he refers to as "the heart of Syria."

—He continually deploys Syrian forces, anti-aircraft missiles and ground-to-ground missile systems in a manner that presupposes conflict.

Upon viewing the Golan Heights first hand, I can more than appreciate the essential need for Israel to defend those heights vigorously because it is one small island of defense between Syria and Israel. With Assad's repeated obsession to pursue a war with Israel, it is quite evident why Jay felt compelled to assist Israel in deterring these very real threats of aggression by her Arab neighbors. Israel stands alone and friendless amidst a region of the world that expresses utter hostility toward her. Certainly, nations such as Syria are no friend of this country. In fact, we believe they have been responsible for overt acts of state-sponsored terrorism directed against U.S. citizens abroad. Again I ask, why is my husband being prosecuted?

I believe that Israel's victories are our wins and her losses are our defeats. Although the prosecution recognizes these facts, the anti-Semites of our government have chosen to turn our case from a legal and moral issue to a political scandal in which they hope to permanently discredit Israel. The prosecution has sacrificed the truth on the altar of political expediency and has virtually shifted our case 180 degrees from the U.S. v. Jonathan and Anne Pollard to the U.S. v. Israel.

Needless to say, this past year has been nothing short of pure, unmitigated hell for both of us. No human being was ever placed on this earth to endure the relentlessly excruciating physical and psychological tortures we have been subjected to. When we visited Yad Vashem, I recall reading a plaque there which said that Jews who sacrificed themselves for the race would be remembered. We never realized that we would fall into this category and become prisoners of Zion. I am convinced that the only reason we have been prosecuted was to send a message to other American Jews with similar inclinations that pro-Israeli sentiments and loyalty in this country will not be tolerated.

Several months ago, *The New York Times* published an article that stated that "former Justice Department officials knew of previous instances in which cases of Israeli spying in the United States were handled without criminal proceedings." Why are we made to be the examples? Furthermore, everyone should ask why were my husband's undertakings necessary? If only the U.S. was as forthcoming with information to Israel three years ago as they are reported to be today, my husband and I would not be in this predicament.

If anything good has resulted from our tragedy, it is that the U.S. is now living up to their [sic] promises to Israel to exchange vital intelligence information critical to Israel's survival.

Prison life has been particularly brutal to us. At first, the prosecutors concocted wild stories that I was a Chinese and Israeli spy in order to secure my wrongful detention for nearly 100 days. I was locked in a tiny, windowless, roach and rat infested cell for 23½ to 24 hours a day. I was deliberately denied essential medical treatment and prescriptions for my numerous health problems, and almost died as a result of this. My hair even turned gray.

I forever listened to the numerous death threats made to me by my fellow neo-Nazi and Moslem inmates as they discussed aloud how they would "kill the dirty Jew bitch."

During my period of incarceration, I was forbidden to speak with anyone and I was not permitted to breath [sic] fresh air nor see the sun. Initially, I was also denied the right to receive reading or writing material, and moreover for the entire period of incarceration, was forbidden to communicate with or see my husband, which is nothing short of torture for a couple as close as we are.

These ghastly restrictions were deliberately designed to either mentally break me or kill me, and I later learned that these restrictions were ordered by high-level government officials, who were outraged over my vow of silence to all law enforcement officials.

Additionally, these officials had hoped that by slowly destroying me, they could convince my husband to cooperate with them. It was a vicious circle that nearly cost me my life.

Members of my family were told by a high ranking prison official that he was extremely concerned about my continued isolated detention under the imposed, atrocious conditions because he had seen "hardened criminals crack in less than two weeks under less tortuous conditions." I had endured it for nearly three months when the official had made this statement.

I was extremely malnourished because of my well known physical inability to digest the greasy high carbohydrate food served there. I subsequently lost nearly 60 pounds. Additionally, I was ridden with untreated, severe abdominal pain which I later learned was exacerbated by my lack of medical treatment and the conditions I was kept under.

Upon my release from jail, I learned that I was suffering from some rare gastrointestinal/biliary disorders in large part because of the authorities' neglect and subsequently underwent major complex surgery in Chicago. The surgeon had performed only 20 other operations nationwide and he was the only surgeon who had ever performed this specialized surgery.

The authorities were well aware of my medical problems, specifically because they had followed my husband and I [sic] to a local hospital where I underwent a surgical procedure the day of my husband's arrest, and out of "concern" had accompanied me home. My physician was questioned by authorities and testified in court about my medical condition, noting that I was scheduled to undergo further diagnostic tests. Additionally, the prosecutors subpoenaed my medical records following my arrest and were well aware of my condition.

My incarceration rivaled those conditions imposed on POWs detained during the Vietnam War. I was often not permitted to have any type of reading material in an effort to pressure me mentally. The sounds I heard included the relentless 24-hour screams of both insane and drug deprived inmates, as well as chatter from the mindless degenerates and constant fighting of street criminals among whom I was surrounded. The odors I smelled were mixed with the unbearable stench of my continually unworkable toilet and sink which prison officials would not fix for days. My skin sweated constantly in the intolerable high-humidity heat. I could not drink the water because it was mixed with sewer gas. I lacked a moment's privacy because I was constantly watched by male and female guards, the male guards especially ogling me whenever I was allowed to take a shower. My closest companions were the families of roaches and other creatures with which I daily awoke to and slept with. The cell was so bare it lacked even sheets and towels. Its horrors continually reminded me of scenes from Poe's "The Pit and The Pendulum." To this day, I wonder how I came out of that jail alive.

Upon my release from jail, the government had left me penniless, unemployed, homeless and friendless. The authorities had seized all of my material and personal valuables including my car, wedding albums, credit cards and check books, as well as my husband's last paycheck. Despite my good reputation in the Washington public relations community, I was blacklisted by both colleagues and friends because the prosecution had branded me as a "spy" and publicly crucified me.

I subsequently took on employment in lower-level positions because they were the only ones available to me. Upon my arrest I was employed as the director of the Washington office of a New York public relations agency that specialized in media training for blue-chip corporations. My career was at a long strived for peak and because of the prosecutors' fervent desire to destroy what little remained of our reputations, I was unhirable in my field. I lost most of my former friends who were afraid to associate with a "spy."

Despite persistent claims from the government that we lead [sic] a "wealthy and luxurious lifestyle," nothing could be further from the truth. It was because of our lack of a luxurious lifestyle and being stripped of employment that we were not able to maintain our modestly priced rented apartment. We not only could not live a luxurious life style, we didn't own any significant possessions such as real estate, a late-model car, a boat, stocks & bonds or even a savings account, "luxurious" items even our prosecutors regularly enjoy. We have never been able to afford these luxuries.

Although my husband and I made comfortable salaries from our respective jobs, the prosecutors also purposely misstated these in their sentencing memorandums and leaks to the press. I am forever reading in the newspapers that we have a $300,000 Swiss bank account. God knows we wish we did because it would certainly solve our financial devastations and legal debts resulting from this ordeal. My legal fees alone are in excess of $100,000. The truth of the matter is that my husband never had access to nor saw a penny of this alleged money. In fact he doesn't even know if any part of it ever existed. I live with daily pressures and harassment from law enforcement officials and the unknown destiny of our future.

Needless to say, I am extremely concerned about my husband's year-long isolated detention and prohibition from communication with anyone outside of myself and his immediate family. These conditions have been extraordinarily hard on him as they are well beyond any reasonable definition of cruel and unusual punishment. Isolation was designed to punish inmates for wrongful behavior within the prison system for up to two weeks. My husband, a kind and gentle man who has been a model prisoner, has endured it for nearly 15 months!

Throughout his incarceration, he has been confined to virtual round-the-clock confinement in a small cage devoid of any human or emotional support. He is continually transferred from one facility to another, never knowing where he'll be from one day to another. The authorities claim that the isolation and frequent moves are imposed because of the ever constant presence of death threats he has received from members of both the Aryan and Moslem brotherhoods. I ask God every day to watch over and protect my husband's sanity and physical well being from these maniacs who run rampant throughout the U.S. prison system.

I recall the recent controversy surrounding France's request that Israel deport a dual national accused of committing murder. His deportation was subsequently prevented because of the argument that his life would have been in danger in French prisons which contain a large Arab inmate population. I wish people would recognize that a Jewish man with publicly known ardent Zionist and pro-Israeli beliefs, who loyally and honorably served our homeland and preserved human life, is anything but safe in an American prison. In addition to the inmates, a man of Jay's background and convictions must equally suspect the prison guards, many of whom immediately despise inmates of higher intelligence, education and professional success, let alone inmates of different races, religions and ideological convictions.

The anti-Semitic atmosphere within the prison system is profuse [sic]. Furthermore, because of the purported death threats against my husband, the prison officials have imposed outlandish visiting restrictions on him. While all other inmates are permitted liberal visits with anyone they desire in the visiting lounge for the entire duration of visiting hours unchained, the authorities have singled Jay out for unconventional treatment. He is only allowed to see only myself, his parents and his sister.

Sometimes we see one another in the visiting lounge, where it has taken the officials up to two hours to escort my husband there, and he is always brought back to his cell earlier than other inmates. We have frequently visited in a cell in the jail itself (I am told I am the only civilian who has ever visited with an inmate inside the jail). These visits are very upsetting to us because we may only see one another for less than an hour under strict supervision, while Jay is chained and shackled like a rabid dog. While I see my husband on nearly every visiting day (he is usually assigned to the Federal Correctional Institution in Petersburg, Virginia, approximately 2½ hours driving time from Washington, D.C.), it tears my heart apart every time I have to leave him. I feel so dreadfully alone without him by my side each day.

Fortunately, the government's erroneous attempt to destroy our marriage was a mammoth mistake. Our profound love and respect for one another has given us the strength to persevere through this ordeal. The government's insatiable zeal to create harm within our relationship was designed to have us turn on one another. Fortunately, as we could have predicted, the government failed miserably, and their contemptible behavior only served to drive us closer together (which for a couple as close as we have always been, seemed impossible, but it happened). I adore Jay and my life has ceased to exist without him by my side. He is the single most important person in the world to me and I long to have our lives return to the same serene, blissful state it was prior to our arrests.

Today, I am kept under virtual house arrest, where I must regularly call and check-in with Pre-Trial Services, U.S. Probation and other law enforcement officials.

We are horrified that the political bigots towards Israel have thus far been permitted to turn our tragedy into a political scandal of such magnitude. We fear that our potential crucifixion at sentencing would ultimately be Israel's, and we pray that these racists will never have their day in court.

My husband and I pray that we will be reunited, permitted to raise a family, and resume productive lives in Israel soon. However I don't believe my actions in any way warrant renouncing my United States citizenship in order to achieve our desired dream.

I deeply appreciate the way you have handled the unforeseen turn of events, and deeply respect your willingness to accept the situation at some public cost to your integrity. Believe me, this is not lost on me and I will do everything in my power to rectify that.

In the meantime, I ask your patience while we evaluate the situation as rapidly as possible. I know that your efforts have already had a profound and beneficial effect for both my husband and myself. Please stay in touch and once again, we are forever grateful to you for your tremendous concern, support and efforts on our behalf.

> Very sincerely yours,
> Anne Pollard

JONATHAN POLLARD'S FIRST
MEMORANDUM TO THE COURT

The following was written by Jonathan Jay Pollard to his attorney in August 1986 as an explanation of what he did and why:

I understand that I am supposed to submit a written version of the offense. The following constitutes my statement which I understand you will present to the court. Issues addressed in this statement include:

(1) The motives and intentions that prompted my involvement with the Israeli Government;
(2) The nature and extent of the knowledge of the Israeli Government concerning my operation;
(3) The effects of the payments on me.

It is my hope that this effort will demonstrate to the court that my ideological convictions, although subsequently corrupted, were genuine and that at no time did I consider undertaking any actions which were directed against the United States Government. It is my belief that the Government of Israel was fully aware of both my assistance to its intelligence services as well as my true motives in this affair, official denials notwithstanding. Having said this I must, nevertheless, take full responsibility for the offense that I committed and offer the following information more as an explanation for my behavior than as an excuse.

(1)

If the past is prologue to the future, then a review of my background would provide a useful insight into the political values and emotional experiences which have shaped my view of the world. For as long as I can remember, Israel has figured prominently in my life both as an object of religious commitment as well as a source of personal strength.

The first flag I could recognize in my early youth was that of Israel and for years our family took quiet pride in my late uncle's decision to provide the fledgling Israeli Army in 1948 with military boots and medical supplies "liberated" from the American Hospital in Paris, which he commanded at the time.

In addition, many of the leading members of the local Jewish community I met while growing up in Texas were also known to have participated in other types of activities that were of critical importance to Israel during its War of Independence, which ranged from the organization of munitions shipments to the acquisition of surplus bombers. For these people the death of Colonel Mickey Marcus, a much decorated West Point graduate, was considered to be emblematic of the lengths to which American Jews should hold themselves personally accountable for Israel's security.

It was always stressed, though, that this extraordinary sacrifice had only been justified by our people's recent trauma during the Holocaust, which suggested that a high level of vigilance and individual commitment was expected from Jews in general and Zionists in particular, in order to ensure the maintenance of Israel's national defense.

Everyone I respected in my adolescence emphasized that American Jews had a special obligation to provide Israel with help because it represented our only insurance against a repetition of the Holocaust in which so many European Jews were trapped without a refuge that would accept them. Indeed, given a recurrent fear within the Jewish community that under the right economic conditions another catastrophe was conceivable even here, the survival of Israel was viewed as nothing less than a racial imperative.

This apocalyptic view was constantly reinforced by relatives who, having somehow escaped the death camps, reminded us that the minute we took the Third Jewish Commonwealth and our acceptance in the Diaspora for granted it was the beginning of the end. A type of subliminal siege mentality was therefore created in which the survival of Israel was portrayed as being essential to our own ethnic security in the United States.

Although this visceral concern felt by American Jews towards Israel usually manifested itself through such legal mechanisms as the donation of money, promotion of emigration, or participation in political lobbying efforts in behalf of the Jewish state in Washington, it was also implicitly recognized that a Zionist could be faced with a situation in which something less overt and possibly of a confidential nature would be expected from him. But just exactly what this might involve was never openly discussed. For example, Jewish homes were expected to be made available for visiting Israelis, who were not to be disturbed for days on end, while Jewish businessmen were routinely used to quietly broker the transfer of sensitive material or processes needed by the Israeli armaments industry.

Despite the cloak and dagger impression left by these descriptions, American Jews were never encouraged or expected to betray the United States or do anything which could possibly hurt this country. It was simply out of the question because American Jews were aware of the indisputable benefits conferred upon them by the vitality of America's pluralistic traditions and global military strength.

My parents never ceased in their efforts to portray this land as a Godsend for Jews, who throughout the course of our long, often tortuous history in the Diaspora, had never experienced a country so full of opportunities and constitutionally enshrined guarantee of religious toleration. It was constantly stressed by every responsible Zionist I encountered that Israel would simply cease to exist in the absence of a democratically secure and geopolitically ascendent United States, which was therefore in the collective self-interest of the various Jewish Diasporic communities to ensure.

To the extent then that Israel's continued viability was inexorably bound up with the fortunes of America, Zionism, as far as I was concerned, did not involve choosing one country over the other. It seemed that an American Zionist could successfully live under the discipline of two nationalisms without facing any potential moral or professional dilemma. This symbiotic view of two parallel, albeit compatible political ideologies, I was later to discover was critically flawed and was far easier to accept in theory than it was in actuality.

The first indication I had that life would be an agonizing struggle between competing values rather than one of coherent academic absolutes occurred when my family moved to Indiana, where I suddenly found myself confronting a community in which racism and bigotry were acceptable social practices. The Ku Klux Klan was well organized in my city having found the climate and soil receptive to its extremist blandishments following a terrible regional economic depression in the early 1960s.

Given the rather unwholesome characteristics of this environment I was never able to establish friendships in my neighborhoods and was compelled to spend most of my time around the city's Hebrew Day School where I felt as least physically safe and emotionally protected. This association lasted six days a week for ten years and involved a highly concentrated curriculum of religious and Zionist indoctrination that regularly stressed the advisability of aliya, or emigration to Israel. Of the 50 children I knew at the school, roughly half left for Israel which is a rate much higher than the national average but, fully understandable within the context of a community that held us collectively responsible for an unemployment rate not of our making.

Jewish children I saw grew up angry and alienated, wishing only to leave and never return. Whatever political conclusions I was forming at the time in terms of our dependence upon the State of Israel for racial survival tended to be confirmed and magnified by my own physical reliance upon such local Jewish institutions and population that existed.

Everything finally came to a climax during the Six Day War in 1967 when I saw for the first time a strong Jewish state successfully defending itself and not simply playing the role of victim. During the days preceding the onset of hostilities, though, our small community was in the grip of depression, fearful that this time Israel's luck, like that of so many other Diasporic groups, had finally run its course. Yet poised on the brink of annihilation, Israel had suddenly exploded across her threatened borders in what appeared to us to be a blinding flash of biblical decisiveness.

The results of the war absolutely astounded us all: the sight of Jewish tanks encamped on the banks of the Suez Canal and our paratroopers praying at the newly liberated Western Wall in Jerusalem was emotionally intoxicating, especially upon those of us who were seriously considering emigration as a viable means of asserting our self worth.

The effect this victory had on me, in particular, can only be imagined and further served to emphasize in my mind the advisability of leaving for Israel where I could put all the humiliations of my adolescence behind me. But my parents were quick to point out that we had as much right to live and work in this country as the next person and that I should not run at the first hint of trouble. They certainly had endured far more institutionalized racism in their lifetime than I had and were able to rise above it, becoming respected members of a sympathetic university community.

However as far as I was concerned, this academic retreat was only an artificial island of calm in a rather inhospitable sea. To their credit, though, my parents persisted and argued that I should stay here, contribute something positive to American society and then decide at some later date about whether I genuinely wanted to emigrate to Israel, equipped with professional skills that would be of use to the state. This was sound advice but, for an impatient child eager to avenge his humiliations, all this did was delay a crisis which was slowly building into monumental proportions. I think it would be accurate to say that this moment was the genesis of my current predicament.

An incredibly poignant visit I paid to Dachau later that summer did nothing to help me resolve this dilemma. As I walked through the camp all I kept thinking about was the similarity of the German Jewish community which all but vanished in the ovens of that facility, with that of my own back in the United States. Despite the unique historical condition that contributed to the rise of the Nazi phenomenon, the German Jews were as culturally assimilated, politically influential and financially secure as the American Jewish community appeared to be, but had still evaporated within the course of ten years.

When I asked myself whether such a genocide could, in fact, happen in America everything I'd experienced growing up tended to confirm my worst fears while all the books on the Holocaust I'd read by such writers as Elie Wiesel, Andre Schwartzbart, Hannah Arendt and Primo Levi were equally pessimistic about man's ability to refrain from such barbaric behavior in the future. As I stood in the ruins of the crematoria it slowly dawned on me that every Jew had a responsibility, an obligation, if you will, to ensure that this nightmare would never happen again.

Emigration certainly seemed to satisfy the requirements of that obligatory service to our race since standing guard on the Golan Heights or along the Jordan River would obviously further the chances of Israel's survival, albeit in a rather small, tactical scale way. But the Holocaust was a macroscopic event which had occurred in the Diaspora. Clearly our communities there demanded protection as well, which no Israeli Army, however large, could adequately provide. There had however been a perceptible change in the attitude of the non-Jewish world towards the Diaspora in the wake of the 1967 victory, which seemed to imply that respect and security could be acquired for our dispersed communities assuming Israel remained militarily supreme in Middle East.

I would have left the camp utterly confused and undecided about the future had I not came to at least the tentative conclusion concerning the contradictory lessons of Dachau and the Six Day War: The only apparent way to prevent the former was to guarantee the latter. My self-imposed obligatory service, then, would be associated with ensuring Israel's security, however ill-defined and nebulous the exact means to that end were at the time.

Unfortunately during the following years, my internal struggle over the question of emigration intensified because of my inability to discover a significant way of contributing to Israel's defense while living in the United States. However I had slowly begun to appreciate the critical role that American Jews played in representing Israel's strategic interests before Washington decision makers and also recognized that my own political horizons were broadening to include a more balanced view of America's global importance.

While visiting Czechoslovakia in the wake of the Soviet invasion that ended Dubcek's experiment with "humanistic communism," I had graphically seen what alternatives there were to the United States and came away absolutely convinced that if the Russians ever succeeded in supplanting America as the premier world power, there would be no future for either Israel or our Diasporic communities.

Once I had developed a more cosmopolitan and less racially myopic understanding of how the world worked, I clearly saw that Israel's ultimate security was a function of how effectively the United States could play the balance of power game with the Soviets. The Russians, who had long been considered evil incarnate by Eastern European Jews, were evidently a common enemy of both the Zionist movement and America, which tended to reinforce my symbiotic view of the two political philosophies.

Therefore, to help Israel was to assist the United States and vice versa. How could it be otherwise? The United States was home to six million of my co-religionists. The thought of doing anything which would in any way jeopardize their security was totally out of the question. Likewise Israel appeared to be America's only dependable ally in the Middle East and was committed to serving as a strategic bulwark against the further spread of Russian influence in that important region of the globe.

As a sister democracy, Israel's value as a role model for the Third World was both indisputable and a source of justifiable pride for American Jews whenever they discussed the basis of the special relationship between Washington and Jerusalem. But of course it was always the military strengths of the Jewish state that people in this country seemed to respect and take for granted if a dependable ally were needed in the Levant to fight either the Russians or their proxies. Israel's military superiority, though, seemed to be a very precarious thing indeed upon closer inspection.

As I gradually developed an expertise in national defense matters at Stanford and The Fletcher School, my understanding of just how much Israel's alleged superiority was dependent upon the availability of timely intelligence was underscored by the surprise attack launched by Egypt and Syria in the autumn of 1973. If the Six Day War established in my mind that Jews could make good warriors, the Yom Kippur War demonstrated just how dangerous a failure of our intelligence services could become. In the space of several hours Syrian armored units had penetrated the Golan defenses and were within shelling range of Tiberias, a Galilee town with a population of 26,000 Jews, some of whom were related to me.

Unlike the experience of 1967, all we kept hearing on the news here was how precarious the margin of Israel success was and that the casualty lists were growing to alarming heights. A call for volunteers went out to permit able bodied men to be transferred from Kibbutzim to the fronts, but the group I was in spent five frustrating days waiting for an El Al flight in Los Angeles before we were told the need for us had passed with Sharon's crossing of the Suez. Although we had won after all, the price had been appalling and I had spent the whole time sitting in an airport terminal 15,000 miles from Israel unable to do anything more than think.

It was during this vigil that I decided the intelligence field would provide me with a skill which would be well received in Israel once

I emigrated. Like Colonel Marcus, I was ready to serve the United States faithfully and then, once I had contributed something to the national defense effort would leave for Israel. The problem with long range plans though is that they very often are overtaken and invalidated by unanticipated events. In my case I quite simply began to enjoy living in the United States and could almost admit that perhaps I would stay here after all. Intellectually at least, I realized that the same effort I expended here to fight the Russians would also indirectly assist Israel. On the other hand, I was utterly lost emotionally since I had prepared myself for so long to emigrate that the thought of remaining and never committing myself physically to the state was incredibly traumatic. So I continued to be in a moral dilemma as to what I should do to help Israel directly.

Merely recognizing that a contiguity of interests existed between our homeland and the United States was not sufficient to quiet the doubts in my mind about the propriety of living safely in the materialistically affluent West while the Israelis were sacrificing their hard won economic gains on the altar of Mars. I still harbored desires to emigrate immediately, but did not want to callously abandon my parents, who had tried so desperately to provide me with an alternative perspective on the Diaspora.

My dilemma took on the characteristics of an obsession and the harder I tried to resolve it the more elusive a solution became. This inner turmoil intruded into my social and academic life to such an extent that at times I just wanted to pack my bags and move to Israel. On several occasions I did make preparations to emigrate, but the thought of what this would do to my parents eventually stopped me. The net results of this unstable situation were incomplete studies, fantasies, a failed engagement and a totally unjustified belief that my parents bore some of the responsibility for my problems, since they didn't encourage emigration. I seemed to be stuck between my passion for Israel and my very real love for this country which suddenly appeared as two mutually exclusive beliefs.

Although I finally made a tentative compromise to remain in the United States, in order to rationalize my indecision, as time passed I just continued to sink ever deeper into a spiritual no-man's land. And as with all borders, be they physical or cerebral, it is the sense of conflicting allegiances that causes the most confusion for an individual who feels he might be living under the burden of a double standard.

The psychological hallmarks of divided loyalties were certainly there for all to see: the uneasy conscience, the sense of personal failure. I was becoming a weak man with good intentions and doomed by pride, which was a condition that perhaps had more in common with classical tragedy than with Jewish melodrama.

However self pity was something I don't think I ever knowingly cultivated at that time because it denied the possibility of a solution to my crisis. Despair though was the price I paid for setting myself an impossible aim. It is, I was once told, the unforgivable sin, but it is a sin I believe that the corrupt or evil man never practices. He either has hope or a very short memory.

Unfortunately my level of desperation increased dramatically when I started working for Naval Intelligence seven years ago. Although I had been cautioned by many of my Jewish friends about the unhealthy atmosphere which reportedly permeated the office, I was totally unprepared for the level and extent of the anti-Semitism which was tolerated within the organization. I tried many times to understand what was behind the deprecating comments and the biased stereotypes but, in the end, I came to the conclusion that the U.S. Navy, like many other naval establishments around the world, was the last refuge of the patrician bigot. People were routinely expressing attitudes towards Israel which were barely distinguishable from those I had heard about Jews while growing up in Indiana, without being reprimanded or even cautioned.

Moreover despite the commonly held belief that the U.S. provides "everything" to the Israelis, the intelligence exchange from the Navy, at any rate, is anything but equitable. I participated in two official intelligence conferences with the Israelis and was amazed to see how high level directives about releasing certain types of information to Jerusalem were routinely shelved by the men in the trenches, who felt that the "Jews" didn't need to know anything.

For example, one analyst when asked for releasable information on Soviet chemical warfare agents turned to me laughing and said that he thought the Jews were overly sensitive about gas due to their experiences during the Second World War and suggested that they should just calm down a bit. The underlying attitude of many of the American participants in these meetings was overtly racist, which produced a corresponding degree of anger and distrust on the part of the Israelis, most of whom felt that their country's security concerns were being totally overlooked.

The principal instruction I received from my superior was that we should only be prepared to give the Israelis enough information to get them paranoid but not enough, say, to let them figure out a countermeasure to a newly identified Soviet weapon system. When I carefully asked how they were expected to cope with all the state-of-the-art Russian equipment pouring into the region, the response was that all they had to do was lose a few planes and then they'd know what radar frequencies to jam.

As can be imagined, it was very difficult for me to work in this kind of atmosphere and not become frustrated at what I thought was an unbelievably cynical view towards Israel's survival. The Israelis were providing everything they had acquired at great personal risk to many of their agents and the navy bureaucrats couldn't care less about reciprocating in an equally open handed manner, as per their instructions. Even Judge Sofaer, head of the State Department's legal affairs department, remarked during one of his recent trips to Israel that there had apparently been a rather large discrepancy between the amount of information which had been authorized for release to Israel and what had actually been made available. In retrospect, if I had only reported what I'd seen to the Navy's Inspector General, this anomalous situation might have been rectified through channels, without me feeling compelled to take matters into my own hands.

Instead I watched the threats to Israel's existence grow and gradually came to the conclusion that I had to do something:

(CENSORED)

a veritable flood of other Soviet equipment was quietly entering the region unnoticed by the Israelis, who were depending upon the U.S. intelligence community for warning of such activity.

Then the bombing of the U.S. Marine Corps barracks in Beirut took place. As I stood in the back of National Cathedral listening to the memorial service for the fallen soldiers it all seemed so senseless—over 200 dead men and all the U.S. Government could do was respond with an ineffectual air raid in which more Americans were killed,

(CENSORED)

The thought struck me that if the government were unwilling to defend its own interests in the Middle East against a type of threat which could be targeted with public support, then it would be unreasonable to assume that the Israelis could be assured of adequate assistance in the event the tide of battle turned against them. I had already seen how one branch of the intelligence community was consistently undermining Israel's ability to prepare for war, while the various Arab powers were receiving what seemed to be a constant stream of Soviet Bloc and Western European military equipment and intelligence information about Israel. The situation had all the characteristics of a sell out in which Israel would face the combined power of her numerous opponents alone, without the benefit of even one reliable ally.

What I couldn't understand was why people didn't see that without Israel the U.S. strategic position in the Eastern Mediterranean was completely untenable and would deteriorate if a war erupted over the area's oil resources with the Soviets. However, assuming Israel's military position could be assured, not only would my homeland be preserved but the United States would benefit directly by having a secure regional base of operations which the Russians could never hope to match.

In this rather emotionally overheated atmosphere I walked out of the memorial service committed to doing something that would guarantee Israel's security even though it might involve a degree of potential risk and personal sacrifice. I knew what I was contemplating was wrong but at the time all I could see was that the ends justify the means. As with many cases of situational ethics, the individual's most difficult hurdle is to accept the fact that the contemplated action, while apparently compelled by a power beyond his control, was still a matter for which he would be held personally accountable. There could never be any excuse which would absolve him of guilt, only explanations which might provide a motivational guide to his crime.

Having made this decision I could admit to its blatant dishonesty, but never its disloyalty. What I thought I'd done was resolve my dilemma in a way which would permit me to work in the Diaspora against the Russian menace while helping Israel at the same time. When I walked through Yad Vashem, the memorial to the Holocaust in Jerusalem, last summer, I was able to look into those countless lost faces staring out of the faded pictures and know, for once, that I had kept faith with them. Nobody will convince me that I had to become a traitor in order to feel this way. With my eyes shut and not fully aware of the consequences, I entered the territory of lies without a passport for return.

From the start of this affair I never intended or agreed to spy against the United States. A review of the documents collected, as well as the results of FBI polygraphs bear out this statement. It was my plan to provide such information on the Arab powers and Soviets that would permit the Israelis to avoid a repetition of the Yom Kippur War in which they were confronted with nothing less than a technological Pearl Harbor. Given the nature of Israeli defense planning, a situation comparable to 1973 will not be tolerated and, in the absence of reliable intelligence identifying the actual capabilities of newly introduced Eastern Bloc equipment, could result in a very destructive preventive war. It should be realized that for a country like Israel, which is actually sensitive to casualties, constrained by limited resources and saddled with highly vulnerable borders, the appearance of a new enemy weapon system on the frontier could mean the difference between a quick surgical campaign and a Pyrrhic victory. Therefore the earlier Israeli military planners know the technical parameters of a given system the faster they can apportion scarce funds to determine suitable countermeasures, many of which are subsequently turned over to the United States for its own use.

The key to this rational approach to the national defense is to have a sufficiently long lead time for the various research establishments production plants, intelligence agencies and operations bureaus to create the requisite hardware and applicable tactics needed to defeat, say, a new Soviet surface-to-air missile (SAM) system. While it is true that the U.S. is providing a great deal of highly classified material to the Israelis, particularly on these weapons, the information is not detailed enough to allow the Israelis to truly understand the nature of the future threat facing them. Without this type of information, there could be a possibility that the Israeli Air Force might not have indisputable command of the air in the opening days of a war in the Golan Heights and with the distance so short to Israeli population centers, ground forces would have to be left alone to fight costly blocking actions until that time when the air force could decisively intervene. For this reason, much of the material I passed to the Israelis concerned both current and projected Soviet SAM technology, its associated electronic warfare devices and command/control/communications systems.

Of all the threats which Israel is currently facing, those represented by the Soviets and their Syrian allies are by far the greatest due to the unpredictable nature of the Assad regime and the publicly acknowledged promise made by Moscow to guarantee Syria's strategic parity with Israel. The undisclosed objective of that parity though is to allow the Syrian armed forces to mount an unannounced "standing start" offensive, designed to wrest control of the Golan Heights and Galilee before the Israelis can mobilize. At the very least, the information I provided the Israelis should permit them to cope with most of the all-important Soviet air defense weaponry that the Syrians are relying upon to provide their invasion forces with a mobile umbrella against Israeli air attack. Assuming those air defenses can be quickly neutralized, the Israelis should be able to contain the Syrian attack as close to the frontier as possible. It should also be remembered that those same Syrian air defenses shot two U.S. Navy jets out of the sky four years ago over Lebanon and are the main reason why the current administration would avoid retaliating against Damascus even if the "smoking gun" of a terrorist incident could be traced back to Mr. Assad's office. Moreover, in the event that the 6th Fleet does require Israeli assistance for additional air support in the eastern Mediterranean against the Russians or Syrians, it's going to be very thankful that the Israeli Air Force will be able to handle the threat environment—without the waste of time associated with "losing a few planes first."

Apart from Syria, I also provided the Israelis with critical strategic information pertaining to their outer rings of enemies: namely, Libya, Algeria, Iraq and Pakistan. The threats represented by these "rejectionist front" states are no less real than those from Syria

(CENSORED)

Although I was rather surprised at the degree of assistance the Israelis needed, it taught me a very good lesson about how the popularly held perceptions of Israel's intelligence collecting capabilities can be totally misleading. They are not by any means an all-knowing giant straddling the Middle East and have been forced to concentrate their best human and technical assets against Syria, which represents the most immediate threat to their survival.

As I slowly came to appreciate the fact that I was providing the bulk of the information reaching Israel on its distant opponents the magnitude of their precarious position dawned on me:

(CENSORED)

Everything I seemed to show them was like adding stones on top of a man desperately trying to remain afloat in shark infested waters and as each new revelation confronted them with seemingly insurmountable problems another one arose to replace it. At times it seemed as if I were becoming the traditional messenger of bad tidings, sowing the intelligence equivalents of the proverbial dragon's teeth.

But their needs were understandably insatiable and as the urgency of their requests took on an almost infectious quality, my whole life seemed to be driven by a fear of overlooking something that might ultimately prove catastrophic. Literally everything I showed them set off alarm bells, particularly those things pertaining to nuclear and chemical warfare advances in the Arab world. With the Iraqis employing nerve agents with impunity in the Persian Gulf War, the Israelis were justifiably concerned about the Syrians' intentions to use such weapons on the Golan Heights—as it now seems likely they will. Needless to say, it takes years to prepare troops and civilian population centers to exist in this type of battlefield environment and the Israelis usually operate on a much shorter time frame than that.

Despite the frenetic pace of the collection effort, though, I appreciated why it was so important to provide as much material as possible. I was quite literally Israel's eyes and ears over an immense geographic area stretching from the Atlantic to the Indian Ocean. Although my responsibility was overwhelming at times, I was more than "adequately" motivated both by my ideological convictions and sense of outrage over terrorist incidents, which the world seemed to accept with equanimity as long as the only casualties were Jews. The reaction in my office to the *Achille Lauro* incident in which an elderly Jewish man, who also happened to be an American citizen, was brutally murdered bordered on the comic.

Perhaps the most direct role I played in helping to eradicate this terrorist threat to humanity occurred in the fall of 1985 when the Israelis decided to raid Yasser Arafat's headquarters outside Tunis. As I understood it, the retaliation was targeted specifically against the PLO's Force 17 Group, which had been responsible for the murder of three defenseless Israeli civilians at a marina located in the Cypriot port of Larnica. I spent two hectic weeks collecting information pertaining to [Tunisia's] air defense reporting system and the PLO's disposition of anti-aircraft weapons, which evidently contributed significantly to the mission's success. It should be kept in mind that the same Force 17 had also killed three U.S. Ambassadors over the past decade with total impunity and was in the process of organizing additional terrorist acts against American diplomatic interests abroad when the Israeli air strike destroyed its command organization. As far as I was concerned this constituted a perfect example of when I thought my actions were of service to both Israel and the United States which, at the time, seemed unable or unwilling to protect its own citizens overseas.

In addition to my "conventional" intelligence gathering activities on behalf of the Israelis, I was also asked for advice on several of their on-going defense projects. These included determining the feasibility of a small trans-atmospheric reconnaissance platform,

(CENSORED)

and suggesting which armaments might prove effective at protecting Iran's Kharg Island oil loading installation from Iraqi air attack. With respect to the latter, it should be understood that even though Iran's clerical leadership is adamantly opposed to Israel's existence, the defeat of the Iranian armed forces in the current Persian Gulf War would leave Iraq free to redeploy a large number of units either to the Golan Heights or Jordan River Valley, thereby compounding the threat to Israel's eastern border. Put in more biblical terms, Israel's interest in Iran's continued viability is a modern day version of "the enemy of my enemy is my friend."

Although this line of reasoning may not on first sight seem

acceptable to many Americans, who are accustomed to a more idealistic foreign policy, it is a little known tenet of U.S. strategic policy that the territorial integrity of Iran must be maintained so as to prevent a vacuum from arising, which could facilitate a Soviet advance to the Indian Ocean. I'm sure Churchill no more enjoyed dealing with Stalin during the Second World War than I did recommending appropriate defensive armaments for Iran, but the logic of realpolitik often require a person to choose between the lesser of two evils. For me, the need to keep the Iraqi regime preoccupied fighting a militarily strong Iran on battlefields far removed from the Israeli frontier was paramount if the delicate strategic balance between Damascus and Jerusalem were to be maintained.

Finally lest there be any confusion over why I provided information on Saudi Arabia and Egypt, it should be appreciated that both countries represent latent threats to Israel which no amount of propaganda to the contrary can alter.

(CENSORED)

The diplomats might have signed the Camp David Accord, but the Egyptian General Staff is still calculating how best to fight a war in the desert wasteland of the Sinai Peninsula. As for Riyadh, apart from the incredible expansion of the Tabok military-industrial complex,

(CENSORED)

the Saudis have been openly providing Syria with over 90% of the hard currency needed for arms from the Soviets. However no information was provided that either dealt with joint U.S.-Egyptian or U.S.-Saudi military exercises, diplomatic agreements or secret military contingency plans.

As I previously stated, I had absolutely no intention of spying on the United States or to provide any critical national defense information to a belligerent. At no time did I ever compromise the names of any U.S. agents operating overseas, nor did I ever reveal any U.S. ciphers, codes, encipherment devices, classified military technology, the disposition and orders of U.S. forces, war fighting plans, secret diplomatic initiatives and obligations, classified organizational wiring diagrams or phone books, vulnerability of nuclear stockpiles or communications security procedures. In addition, I did not put any U.S. covert activity in jeopardy which might, if compromised, either be used to embarrass the administration or cause a rupture in relations with a foreign government.

One has to keep in mind the fact that my sole objective in this affair was to provide Israel with information concerning threats to its existence, of which the United States is clearly not one. The collection effort was clearly directed against the Soviets and those Arab states which pose a clear and present danger to Israel's security.

On the other hand, if I had intended to harm the United States, I don't think there was anything preventing me from doing so. Although I was ideally placed to acquire nearly any type of information which would be of importance to a belligerent, this thought never crossed my mind. The notion that I was a traitor or working on something which would harm the United States never arose since the agreed upon ground rules of the operation clearly stipulated that I would never be asked to provide material which would put my loyalty to this country in question.

This point was repeatedly stressed by all the Israelis with whom I was associated except Rafi Eitan, who did press me for information pertaining to the activity of the National Security Agency in Israel and the names of all the Israelis who were providing classified information to the United States. I never provided this type of information and was later told by my chief handler, Yosef Yagur, that the material Eitan wanted was totally off limits, outside the scope of the operation, and if provided would be grounds for immediately terminating our relationship.

In the final analysis, the value of the material I provided the Israelis actually goes far beyond the immediate tactical advantage it will confer upon their field commanders: by giving high level Israeli defense planners a detailed look at the nature of their future threat environment, it permits the country's political leadership to articulate an external policy based on certainties rather than debatable risks.

This advantage would tend to work as a stimulant for the peace process since no responsible Israeli government could ever consider yielding valuable territory unless it had an accurate assessment of what the potential loss to the nation's military security would be from such a decision. Although I'd be the first one to overstate the degree of danger Israel is currently facing, I also appreciate the fact that a time for peace, even an imperfect "cold one," must inevitably be accepted before the state is transformed into a Prussian clone. I am satisfied that what I did will hasten the day that peace can be reached in the region because without much of the information I provided, the Israeli military establishment would be less inclined to trust the assurances of its own political leadership, let alone those of a traditional enemy.

In conclusion, during the course of this affair I tried to remain truer to my ideological convictions—as imperfect and flawed as they might have been in retrospect. In my mind assisting the Israelis did not involve or require betraying the United States. I never thought for a second that Israel's gain would necessarily result in America's loss. How could it? Both states are on the same side of the geopolitical barricade.

(2)

One of the most controversial aspects of this case has been the assertion by the Israeli Government that it had no prior knowledge either of my activities on their behalf or of the allegedly unauthorized behavior of their own intelligence operatives. Before addressing this contention, it should be pointed out that whereas a state's decision to conduct espionage against a belligerent is a routine phenomenon, this affair represents a highly unusual situation involving two closely aligned nations, one of which felt compelled to spy indirectly on its enemies through the services of an allied national.

Although this embarrassing type of discovery has previously occurred, both parties very often resolved their differences quietly through diplomatic or administrative channels, neither state wishing to precipitate a cause célèbre, which might put at risk more substantive aspects of their relationship. It is my belief that if this imbroglio had been managed in such a discrete [sic] manner, the Israeli Government might have been more inclined to act responsibly from the start and to quickly admit their culpabililty. Candor, however, is a rather scarce commodity in shaky coalition governments, particularly one just waiting for a crisis to disintegrate—and this case was a crisis of monumental proportions for Israel, comparable in some respects to the Lavar affair over 25 years ago. In response to the blistering public denunciations which were directed at it, the Israeli government acted predictably by attempting to limit the damage to itself by retreating behind a plausible denial screen in which the scandal was purportedly precipitated by a group of renegade intelligence officers acting without authorization. Once having engaged in this self-defeating approach to the problem, the Israelis were vulnerable to additional embarrassment as each new uncontested revelation was prominently displayed in the American media. Perhaps sometime in the future a more politically secure Israeli government will be able to set the record straight with the U.S. Department of Justice, but until that day arrives it will be more expedient for Israel's fractured leadership to stonewall and deny any official involvement with my activities. However having said all this, the following represents my understanding of the government's knowledge of the operation.

First of all, the number and type of Israelis who were associated with this affair suggest a high degree of government awareness if not intimate supervision of their behavior. Given both the comparatively small size of the Israeli intelligence community as well as its notorious infra-service volubility, the plausibility that seven members could carry out a "renegade" operation unbeknownst to security and fiscal management personnel is beyond reason. Even with the availability of a bureaucratically unaccountable "slush" fund, the expenses of this operation could not have passed unnoticed by the Inner Cabinet's intelligence auditor, who has an extremely broad mandate for regulating these sensitive financial outlays. Furthermore if one takes into account both the quality and highly specialized professional expertise of the personnel who were involved in this affair, it seems unlikely that their collaboration could have been the product of random selection: a near famous ex-Mossad assistant chief of operations, then assigned as a special advisor to the Prime Minister, a highly decorated member of the Air Force, two senior science attachés, and a leading international arms broker do not simply coalesce out of thin air.

Secondly, the type of collection guidance I received suggested a highly coordinated effort between the Navy, Army and Air Force intelligence services. At the end of each month, I was given an extremely detailed list of material which was needed by the various organizations that included an explanation of why the information officially transferred did not satisfy their requirements. Although the acquisition lists appeared to have been submitted by each service separately, since dissimilar plans and formats were used by the three organizations, there was always one prioritized list which had evidently been agreed upon by the respective military chiefs of intelligence and bore their combined seal. While it is possible that the Mossad considered this affair to have been "unauthorized" because they were evidently never a party to it, the same cannot be said of the General Staff, which was intimately involved with identifying which type of scientific and technical intelligence was to be the object of my activity. From what I could see, Rafi Eitan only served as the individual responsible for managing the covert side of this uniformed service operation.

Thirdly, I was routinely provided with finished technical assessments of the material which had been passed to the Israelis. The turn around time for these assessments was very quick and when I inquired how this was accomplished was told that a special team of analysts had been established back in Israel just for the purpose of evaluating the operational applicability of all the new information collected. Given the unique nature of this material, such as satellite photography and SIGINT-derived studies (CENSORED) this team was not only fully aware of when the information was being acquired, but was also cognizant that it was not being transferred through official channels. Although I was never told how large this group was, it had to have been rather well staffed with extremely competent scientists in light of the volume and diversity of the material I collected.

Fourthly, there were three occasions on which I was told that the higher levels of the Israeli government had purportedly extended their collective thanks for the assistance I had provided the state. After I had supplied Yosef Yagur with a very detailed study of Pakistan's facility, he informed me that a special studies committee, directly subordinated to the Prime Minister's office, had presented its conclusions to the Cabinet on the growing dangers of the Pakistani weapons effort and had emphasized, in writing, that the intelligence material obtained from a "special source" had been critical to its evaluation. I was also congratulated by Yagur after an Israeli drone, or unmanned reconnaissance aircraft, had been able to successfully negotiate its way through the entire Syrian air defense system in 1985. According to the Israeli Air Force, this remarkable achievement was only possible due to the material I provided

Lastly, after the raid on the PLO headquarters on the outskirts of Tunis, both Yagur and Colonel Sella stressed the fact that the mission could not have been undertaken without the information I made available to the staff preparing the operation. Once again, reference to Israel's dependence upon a "special source" was reportedly mentioned at the pre-strike presentation made before the Cabinet.

Fifthly, since Eitan was physically located in the Prime Minister's office and was evidently involved in some type of intense bureaucratic competition with the Mossad, it is very likely that he provided both my name and position to the select group of Israeli politicians and General Staff representatives who would have been briefed on the agent responsible for such intelligence coups as the photos of Pakistan, the aerial romp over Syria and the raid against the PLO's North African headquarters. The inner Cabinet would have wanted to know who provided this information and Eitan could never have resisted the opportunity to score points against the Mossad in front of the government. Yagur mentioned several times that specific documents had been used by Eitan to embarrass the Chief of Mossad at Cabinet meetings and, as stated earlier, the material was so unique that anyone present at the carefully orchestrated confrontations would have known about the existence of an agent working in the American intelligence establishment.

For whatever reason, a Cabinet level decision had to have been made, with the concurrence of the General Staff, that the gains associated with my activities far outweighed any potential risks that might result if I were compromised. After all, incidents had happened in the past and there was no reason to believe that the American government would react any differently in my case, especially as I was not spying on the United States. The opinion that I had nothing to fear in the event of capture was stressed to me by both Yagur and Eitan so often that it seemed as if they were repeating official dogma. It is my opinion that they were, but that with the affair exploding out of control following my arrest, the opportunity was seized by certain factions in the Cabinet and the Israeli intelligence community to repudiate the operation by casting Eitan in the role of a renegade. I don't know whether anyone in

the Israeli leadership was aware of the fact that Eitan had unsuc-
cessfully attempted to have me collect political blackmail on members of the Cabinet but, assuming someone did, there would have
been an incentive to publicly discredit both him as well as myself
before he had a chance to leak such inflammatory information.
Politics in Israel has certain Byzantine characteristics, which to the
outsider, may appear to be self-destructive. It is indeed unfortunate
that this political trait has also served to destroy an otherwise loyal
Zionist and discredit the reputation of a sitting Israeli government.

(3)

Of all the corruptive influences which are popularly viewed as
being decisive in prompting an otherwise law abiding man to
become a spy for a foreign government, sex, drugs and money are
considered to be the most potent. The fact that this "trinity of evil"
has been evident in many of the espionage cases which have come
to light over the past few years makes any claim of ideological
conviction by me to appear self serving at best and irrelevant at
worst. However the minute one automatically ascribes greed as the
principal motive in affairs such as mine, it tends to obscure the
more fundamental issues which can render a person vulnerable to
his ideological obsessions. Although I never sold my soul to Mammon, it is extremely frustrating for me to see that only the financial
aspects of my involvement with the Israelis seems to have captured
center stage, particularly in terms of our alleged life style, trips and
subsidies. Contrary to what the novelist may say is the "spark of
deceit," money was a corruptive secondary by-product of my activities and was certainly not the preceptory or causative agent.

When I first made contact with Colonel Sella and offered my
services to the Israelis, I never intended to establish a business
relationship with them. My sole objective was to provide the Israeli
Defense forces with enough information for the next generation of
Soviet military technology which had been scheduled for export to
the Middle East. Accordingly I worked as an Israeli agent for nearly
six months without receiving any monetary compensation and was
content to continue this arrangement until the issue of salary was
raised by Colonel Sella. At first I did not know how to respond to
this situation since I hadn't planned on being paid for my assistance, believing instead that if I were to successfully complete

the transfer of intelligence data the Israelis would permit me to work for one of their defense industries in the United States or Europe, such as Israel Military Industries, Tadiran, or Israel Aircraft Industries—where I could continue to aid the state as an armaments marketing strategist. However seeing to the fact that I wasn't even familiar with the type of salary an agent could reasonably expect, some ridiculous amounts were initially discussed until I understood that Eitan intended to pay me as if I were a regular agent operating in "friendly" territory. As he explained it, nobody would question a CIA operative living off two salaries when he's employed overseas by an unknowing firm as deep undercover and the same logic applied for me as an Israeli operative.

I still didn't like the situation that was developing and discussed alternative forms of compensation with Sella, Yagur and Eitan while in Paris during the winter of 1984. I suspect that the best way of characterizing the way I felt at the time was extremely dirty, which was not how I envisioned feeling as a result of helping the Israelis. This was an ideological operation that was slowly being turned into a banking expedition by Eitan. Both Yagur and Sella privately agreed with me that the payments would be misinterpreted and look terrible if I were arrested and suggested to Eitan that Anne be employed by a sympathetic public relations firm instead. Eitan, predictably, adamantly refused to consider anything other than a salary and emphasized that as an Israeli working for him I was expected to follow orders and proceed with my collection activity. Every time Yagur passed money to me a silence would descend over our discussions and a rather pained look would appear on his face. There was one occasion where I did refuse to accept the money, but Yagur pointed out that it was not up to me to lecture a man like Eitan on ethics—what we were involved with was a matter of critical importance for our homeland and insubordination in the field would not be tolerated. There was no denying the fact, though, that neither one of us fully enjoyed the salary aspect of our operation, which conveniently hung like a sword of Damocles over my head.

In spite of this disquieting aspect of my case, I never considered myself to be a mercenary, no matter how corrosive the payments were on my sense of personal integrity. Luckily, my ideology prevented me from descending to a level where I would reflexively respond to Eitan's commands, like some type of Pavlovian dog. As

I've previously mentioned, when he requested information which I considered to be incompatible with my objectives and intentions I simply did not provide the material. It might be instructive to remember that unlike most mercenaries, I had no blackmail threat which could be directed against me. In fact, the classical roles of compromised agent and manipulative handler were actually reversed in this affair and if any party were vulnerable to extortion, it was the Israeli Government, which politically had a great deal to lose if my activities were discovered. Therefore if I were simply motivated by greed, I should have exacted a King's ransom for my services each time a delivery was made to the Israelis. That I did not demand an increasing amount of money during this operation should indicate that my ideological convictions were fundamentally genuine.

When all is said and done though, I did accept money for my services. That fact has a way of suggesting the worst kind of motive in a spy, a species not generally well regarded to begin with. Yet even idealistically inclined spies cannot exist on altruism or sheer stamina for very long because of the rate at which they tend to deteriorate from fear, exhaustion, and a guilty conscience. Unlike an agent operating behind enemy lines, I knew what I was doing was wrong and constantly tried to keep my spirits up by reminding myself that the information I was providing Israel was essential to its survival. But in the absence of any conventional yardstick by which I could determine my absolute worth to the state, I accepted the payments as a reflection of how well I was doing my job.

By the spring of 1985, Eitan felt that it was time to recognize the quality of the material being collected and awarded me a salary increase which I received without any discussion: Yagur handed me an envelope, we shook hands, he apologized and I felt like a prostitute. Finally, after a year of rising emotional distress over this financial stigma, I wrote to Eitan informing him that I not only intended to repay all the money I'd received but, also, was going to establish a chair at the Israeli General Staff's Intelligence Training Center outside Tel Aviv. When I later apprised Colonel Sella about my decision he smiled and said that Eitan would very likely have a case of apoplexy upon receipt of the message since he couldn't stand agents who suffered from "morality attacks." Ironically the only response I ever got from Eitan was transmitted through *The Jerusalem Post,* shortly after my arrest, where he evidently felt obliged to characterize me as a mercenary. Like the 18th century Bourbons, Mr. Eitan seems to know the price of everything and the value of nothing. I am at least relieved to know though, that Yagur has refuted this spiteful comment as being totally inaccurate.

When I was first asked how the money provided by the Israelis affected our life style, I could only respond by pointing out that we didn't acquire such ostentatious items as property, cars, furniture, electronic equipment, furs, paintings, gold, stock, boats, racing horses or, for that matter, a drug habit. Before I became involved with the Israelis, we were meeting our rent payments and other household expenses while the apartment was fully furnished and the car was paid off. This financial situation would have continued indefinitely seeing to the fact that we were managing our money responsibly and were not profligate in our spending patterns.

The extra funds did however permit us to travel to Europe on two occasions during which time I also met with my Israeli contacts for debriefing sessions. The hotels we stayed at, the restaurants we enjoyed and our modes of transportation were well beyond what a couple on our salaries could normally have afforded. Some aspects of those trips were subsidized immediately by the Israelis, while other portions were to be paid off slowly over the course of a year with funds taken from my monthly payments. There was also the matter of Anne's ring which was part of the plan to convince her that a wealthy relative was underwriting our trip to Europe at the time—it was certainly not meant to be a recurrent aspect of my relationship with the Israelis. As far as the Swiss bank account was concerned, that was presented to me by Eitan as a means of addressing my stupid concern over his lack of adequate security precautions. It was his contention that even though I had absolutely nothing to fear in the event of compromise, the bank account would serve as a safety net in the unlikely event we had to relocate overseas at the end of ten years. It was definitely not established to supplement my monthly payments and could not even be accessed without authorization from Yagur, who had opened the account in my Israeli name. The ten year time period was Eitan's invention and was clearly unreasonable, since I had already made the decision to terminate my activities at the end of 1985. When I broached this matter with both Yagur and Sella, they each recognized that ten years was untenable because of my growing dissatisfaction with Eitan's reduction of everything in the relationship to an accounts ledger. The possibility of me actually working for Eitan long enough to collect $300,000 was therefore a non-starter and simply never would have occurred.

It may be relevant to place the recovered letter to Yossi I wrote within the context of this financial situation. As previously alluded to, Israel is committed to maintaining Iran's conventional military capabilities in order to assure a stalemate in the Persian Gulf War. Since the U.S. has repeatedly warned Israel in the past against openly shipping arms to Iran, the Israelis have very conveniently delegated this activity to trusted private brokers, who can also be repudiated if exposed. This policy decision communicated to me involved the following issue, which "Uzi" had been assigned to expedite: Kharg Island's defenses were to be improved before Iran opted to close the entire Persian Gulf oil flow off in retaliation for Iraq's increased number of air strikes against the facility. My suggestions were solicited as to how that objective could be realized given the fact that I was in the best position to know exactly what weapons the Iraqi Air Force was using to interdict the oil loading complex. The understanding was that since I would eventually be employed either in the official or "gray" arms market, this assignment could be viewed as my initiation, commission and all. This proposed sale of military equipment to Iran was no more an isolated "rouge" [sic] affair than was the operation in which I was involved—both were authorized activities which formed an essential part of Israel's survival oriented strategy. The commission was unanticipated and had no affect on my predisposition to provide the information Israel needed to successfully conclude an arms deal with Iran—the objective of this endeavor was always of foremost importance to me, not the profit.

With respect to our alleged penchant for frequenting expensive Washington restaurants, many of the meals were taken with friends who could reimburse us later for their having used our credit cards and we were always careful to eat during those hours when prix fix (i.e. pre-theater) savings were available. I can't remember one occasion when we ordered wine or offered to pick up the entire tab for a meal involving our friends. In fact, most of our favorite restaurants were small Greek, Italian, or Vietnamese establishments which were modestly priced and provided us the opportunity of quick inexpensive meals after very long, exhausting days at work. Anne and I patronized those restaurants long before I started working for the Israelis and would have continued doing so even without an additional monthly paycheck.

Although Anne's job required her to be dressed appropriately, I can't recall a single time she ever purchased anything that wasn't on sale. Moreover due to her frequent and painful weight problems, caused by a number of gastrointestinal disorders, she was forced to buy clothes that would fit her properly across a broad spectrum of sizes. A certain percentage of the money was used for educational expenses, prescription medications, and books for which I will be the first to admit I have an incurable addiction. The extra money also permitted us to attend two weddings in Portland, Maine, and Tampa, Florida, which I don't think we would otherwise have been in a position to afford. Although in retrospect our way of life was not dramatically changed because of the Israeli subsidy, it was, nevertheless, significantly improved to the degree that we could do certain things and purchase a few items that were previously beyond our financial reach. This ability did not, by any means, turn us into unbridled sybarites or permit a degree of consumption that would be considered unseemly.

Perhaps the most significant impact my additional funds had on our life was that it provided me with the resources to co-opt a highly placed Saudi bureaucrat. His potential utility for my eventual plan to leave the Navy and initiate a covert penetration of the Saudi Ministry of Foreign Affairs was incalculable. A great deal of money was spent on this project, which would have resulted in a tremendous opportunity for me to work as this bureaucrat's private representative in London and Brussels. Beyond the evident intelligence value of this relationship, it would have allowed me to end my operation in this country, which Yagur had told me in October of 1985 had already provided the Israeli armed forces with enough information to probably win the next Middle East war. Ironically, it was money taken from a commission I earned brokering an oil contract on behalf of the Saudi with which I intended to repay the Israelis for all the funds I had received from them.

This act would not have totally erased the stigma I felt by having accepted their money in the first place, but it would have constituted the first step on the road to my personal redemption. I never imagined that Eitan could have insisted upon these payments as a precautionary move designed to cast me in the unlikely role of a mercenary in case the operation was compromised. It seems that Lucretia Borgia couldn't have recommended a more potent way of poisoning my motives. Luckily my ideological convictions held fast in spite of the money and prevented me from giving Eitan any information which I considered to be outside the scope of our operation. Although the money may have corrupted me by contact, it did not form the basis of my decision to help Israel.

JONATHAN JAY POLLARD'S SECOND MEMORANDUM TO THE COURT

I. INTRODUCTION

Defendant, Jonathan J. Pollard, by counsel, respectfully submits this memorandum in aid of sentencing by the Court. Pursuant to an agreement, Mr. Pollard pled guilty to a single violation of 18 U.S.C. Pp 794(c), the penalty for which may range from any term of years to life imprisonment and/or a fine up to $250,000.

Mr. Pollard previously submitted for the Court's review a statement written entirely by him (and typed for the Court's convenience) explaining his personal background, motivations for delivering information to Israel, and his current feelings toward the crime he committed. An unclassified version of the statement has been filed with the Court as well. Mr. Pollard also submits herewith for the Court's review this classified memorandum containing a detailed explanation of the nature of the documents allegedly compromised by Mr. Pollard, an analysis of the Government's claim of the damage to the United States caused by his actions, and a refutation of several points raised in the Government's memoranda.

II. DAMAGE TO THE UNITED STATES

A. *Introduction*

Perhaps the critical issue in the Court's determination of an appropriate sentence for Mr. Pollard is the extent to which his conduct damaged the interests of the United States. In recognition of the importance of the damage issue, the United States not only devoted a section of its public sentencing memorandum to a discussion of the alleged damage caused by him, but it also has filed a supplement to the memorandum elaborating on its contentions and has submitted an affidavit by the Secretary of Defense purportedly detailing the damage assessment.

While it is proper, indeed, obligatory, that the United States set forth its views regarding damage inflicted by Mr. Pollard's conduct, Mr. Pollard expected that the opinions expressed would be succinct, objective, and relevant. Instead, the United States has filed a blizzard of contentions notable for the emphasis on the phrases "may have," "could have," and "possibly has."

The damage assessment[1] in this case fails to establish the fact of injury in such a way as to justify substantial incarceration for Mr. Pollard. As presented, it is an overstated polemic of the evidence one expects to find in a case of espionage. Instead of concentrating on the actual damage to U.S. national interests, the United States has engaged in unbridled speculation on the potential damage. While this speculation would be germane if Mr. Pollard had only been apprehended yesterday, over fifteen months have elapsed since his arrest. During that time, the United States has debriefed him extensively, conducted exhaustive reviews of the documents delivered by him to the Israelis, and had the opportunity to observe any material alteration of the relationships between it and the government of Israel, allied nations and friendly Arab nations. The United States should have developed a concrete assessment of the damage by now, thereby obviating the need for any speculation. The United States' reliance on speculation therefore underscores the tenuousness of its claims.

B. There Was No Disclosure to the Enemy

In the first place, no injury is demonstrated in the same way as in the case of unauthorized disclosures to a hostile nation. This point comes home only when a comparison is made between which the Government asserted to be the injury to our national security in such celebrated recent cases as Walker, Pelton, and Morison. In each of those prosecutions, the injury to the United States was painfully clear: the Soviets received the classified materials.[2] The result was that sources of information were compromised, secret methods of collection exposed, and locations of equipment and personnel revealed. Since the U.S. intelligence effort is directed primarily at the Soviet Union, these repercussions meant basically that the United States had to start over to reestablish a collection network. Accordingly, the United States was required to establish new communications links, methods and channels, to replace lost equipment and personnel, to find new intercept sites, and to develop new technology to circumvent Soviet defenses or interference.

The Government has argued that the sheer volume of the information provided has made this one of the worst espionage cases in U.S. history. Again, this pandering simply fails to recognize the most salient of all facts in the case: the enemy was not the recipient of the information. Volume *per se* is irrelevant if it is not reflective of injury. As an example, in *U.S.* v. Morison, United States District Court for the District of Maryland, the defendant was convicted and sentenced to 3 years in jail for having supplied *Jane's Defense Weekly* with a satellite photograph of a Soviet ship under construction. Mr. Pollard participated in the damage assessment for the Morison case.

(2½ lines censored)

Thus, the volume of the compromised information meant nothing; it was the Soviet's possession of it that created the injury to our national security.

In this case, no such allegation of such damage is made or proof offered. Secretary Weinberger nowhere alleges that the United States has lost the lives or utility of any of its agents, that it has been obligated to replace or relocate intelligence equipment, that it had to alter communication signals, or that it has lost other sources of information, or that our technology has been compromised. Indeed the memorandum only discusses the *possibility* that sources may be compromised in the future, thus requiring countermeasures. The absence of any countermeasures taken in the aftermath of Mr. Pollard's conduct therefore is perhaps the truest barometer of the actual damage, or absence thereof, to the national security.

Consequently, the methodology of this damage assessment is seriously flawed for lack of a "clincher." Its focus on damage is not in the compromise of the substantive information but rather on the intangible, unproven speculation that we shall be unable to negotiate effectively with the Government of Israel over intelligence sharing for some time. One may assume that if there were evidence of this, it would be presented in these papers. Certainly, after the passage of 18 months since the Israelis began receiving information from Mr. Pollard, such a development would have surfaced by now—if it in fact has happened; it has not.

C. *The Political Impact*

The speculation, in the absence of hard evidence, extends to the Secretary's concern about our allies. Again, there is no showing of any adverse fallout with our allies from these disclosures. Again, with so many months having passed since this case broke, it is reasonable to expect evidence of this adversity and not someone's theoretical notion that it could happen.

Even the political argument is questionable. Is the Israeli Tunis raid different from the U.S. raid on Tripoli? It is not fair or accurate to distinguish the two on the basis of our friendship with Tunisia versus our enmity with Libya. Each was a violation of sovereign territory. Each was carried out for the same purpose: to retaliate against terrorists in their known locations. Each was praised by our President as responsible reactions to terrorism. After 15 months, since Mr. Pollard's arrest, our relations with each of those countries has not changed. Therefore, the Secretary's policy analysis is less an analysis and more a convenient theory of injury which bears no relation to reality.

D. *Israel's Intent in Receiving Classified Information*

By the same token, fears about what Israel might do with this information by sharing it with third countries, are completely unfounded, unless, of course, the Secretary is willing to state that information Israel has lawfully received is also subject to improper sharing. If that is the case, the danger here is not peculiar to the compromised information; it extends to all of it—compromised and uncompromised alike.

The heinousness of any espionage must take into account the intent of the recipient of the classified information to harm the United States. There is no evidence in the damage assessment of Israel's intent to injure the United States by reason of its having illegally received the classified information from Mr. Pollard. Israel is simply not the enemy—it is not the Soviet Union—it is not a Warsaw Pact nation—it is not China—it is not even India. Israel, as it has been pointed out, enjoys a "special relationship" with the United States. It is our staunch, steadfast ally. The worst that has been said about our loss in this case is that our negotiating posture in near term intelligence exchanges might be jeopardized (although after 15 months no evidence of this appears).

There is more psychology at work here than there is injury. Notoriety is the direct result of the much-debated, discussed, and analyzed phenomenon of how loyal Jewish-Americans can serve the ideal of supporting the Jewish state without doing violence to their allegiance to the United States. Mr. Pollard failed to maintain that intellectual and spiritual balance that Jewish-Americans strive to maintain between their love for Israel and their loyalty to the United States. For his actions as a result thereof, he must be accountable to our laws.

E. Relationship between the United States and Israel

Just as a man who strikes another suffers varying degrees of punishment depending on whether the victim lives or dies, so should Mr. Pollard be sentenced on the basis of the damage he caused to the security of the United States. It is clear that punishment must be imposed in the form of incarceration but that does not mean it should be done without regard to the actual harm suffered by the United States in this case. Accordingly, the one point which he asks the Court never to lose sight of is that the country to which he passed classified information was not the Soviet Union. Instead, the recipient of the information is probably one of the closest, if not the closest, ally of the United States. Since Israel's formal establishment in 1948, the United States has provided substantial assistance to it, in the form of military hardware, financial aid, and intelligence information. Even though the United States has never committed formally to defending Israel from aggression, a cornerstone of U.S. foreign policy for almost forty years has been a self-imposed duty to ensure the survival of that nation. To that end, Israel remains the largest recipient of U.S. military equipment and financial aid, even though it is a diminutive country both in size and population.

The relationship between the United States and Israel is not exclusively that of donor-donee. The United States' commitment to the survival of Israel is not entirely a product of altruism. The United States does have a natural sympathy towards Israel because it is the only stable democracy in the Middle East, and because it is surrounded by hostile enemies with larger populations and resources, whom it nevertheless defeated in three wars. However, Israel also has undertaken operations from which the United States derived substantial benefit. In past years, Israel has frustrated numerous terrorist activities against U.S. targets and provided information to be used in U.S. intelligence activities or actions against terrorism.

(5½ lines censored)

Israel has also acted on the United States' behalf when direct U.S. involvement would be politically impossible or detrimental to U.S. foreign policy. For instance, when the United States normalized relations with the People's Republic of China in 1978, the PRC insisted that the U.S. diminish its arms sales to Taiwan. The United States ended direct sales to Taiwan, but Israel, with the encouragement of the United States, became the new supplier of U.S. arms. More recently, the media has been detailing Israel's covert role as a broker of U.S. arms sales to Iran.

Given this extensive and intimate relationship between Israel and the United States, it should not be surprising that the Israeli and U.S. Governments have entered into formal agreements for the exchange of intelligence information. Secretary Weinberger's affidavit admits that pursuant to these agreements a large quantity of intelligence information, much of it highly classified, is disclosed as a matter of policy to the Israelis. Secretary Weinberger insists, however, that the information passed by Mr. Pollard to Israel exceeds the scope of the exchange agreements.

F. Criteria for Dissemination of Information to Israel

An inspection of the criteria the Secretary listed in gauging what information could be disseminated to the Israelis shows that, contrary to Secretary Weinberger's claims, the information Mr. Pollard passed to the Israelis does not undisputedly fall outside those criteria. Secretary Weinberger identifies six criteria used in making the determination whether to share information.

(4 pages censored, i.e., deleted)

Secretary Weinberger repeatedly contends that the information given to the Israelis by Mr. Pollard has damaged U.S. interests in the Middle East. While Mr. Pollard and his counsel lack access to information necessary to refute all of Secretary Weinberger's accusations, some of the assertions are contrary even to established viewpoints in the intelligence community. For instance, Secretary Weinberger insists that a stronger Israel upsets the balance of power in the Middle East and therefore makes armed conflict more likely. If the United States truly believed that, it would not provide Israel with the most sophisticated military equipment and generous foreign aid. Instead, one of the bulwarks of U.S. policy in the Middle East is to ensure that Israel maintains a clear military superiority in the region. As stated in a classified report titled "The Arab-Israeli Military Balance," prepared by the U.S. intelligence community, "the United States sells some of its best and most advanced equipment to Israel on a timely basis, occasionally even before some US forces receive it."*Id.* at 9. The unqualified support which the United States displays for Israel reflects in part a realization that Israel would not initiate a war simply because it thinks it has a military advantage over its enemies. To the contrary, with the knowledge of military superiority, Israel would not experience the insecurity which fuels wars in the Middle East.

(7 lines censored)

Secretary Weinberger attempts to refute his own employees' analysis of the above-described political reality in the Middle East by pointing to the Tunis raid as an example of Israeli aggressiveness prompted by a clear military advantage over its enemies. Secretary Weinberger misses one key distinction. The raid on Tunis was not directed against Tunisia, but was a surgical strike aimed at a terrorist organization. While relations with Tunisia may have been ruffled over the attack (though there was no rupture of ties), it is interesting that President Reagan, architect of U.S. foreign policy, stated immediately after the raid that other nations have the right to strike at terrorists "if they can pick out the people responsible." *World News Digest,* October 4, 1985.[4] In addition, the strike was not a product of new-found intelligence data supplied by

Mr. Pollard, but rather reflected an application of Israel's consistent policy of retaliating for terrorist actions against its nationals. Accordingly, the information which Mr. Pollard supplied undoubtedly furthered the attack, but it did not induce it. Indeed, the information most likely minimized the loss of Israeli and Tunesian [sic] lives, which would be in the best interests of U.S. policy, by permitting a more accurate attack against the PLO headquarters.

G. Damage to Relations with Friendly Arab Countries

Secretary Weinberger's second contention is that U.S. relations with friendly Arab countries have been damaged.

(3 lines censored)

The Israelis assuredly realize that disclosure of the extent of the information received from Mr. Pollard will jeopardize the advantage which the information gives them over their present or potential enemies, since it would spur the enemies to take effective countermeasures.

(8 lines censored)

A related concern of Secretary Weinberger's is that information acquired by Israel through Mr. Pollard's activities could be used against Arab countries in a manner which would damage U.S. foreign policy. Secretary Weinberger again points to the raid against the PLO headquarters in Tunis as evidence of the uses to which the Israelis would put the information and the ensuing damage to U.S. policy. Specifically, Secretary Weinberger contends that U.S. relations with Tunisia have been injured because of that raid. Secretary Weinberger does not indicate, however, whether the damage, if any, which occurred to the bilateral relations was a result of the attack itself or the United States' failure to condemn it immediately. Again, assuming that the raid would have taken place regardless of Mr. Pollard's passing of information to the Israelis, Mr. Pollard may have minimized the damage to U.S.-Tunisia relations by reducing the number of Tunisian fatalities.

Over eighteen months have elapsed since Mr. Pollard began providing information on Arab countries to the Israelis. During that time, Israel has not attacked one Arab country. Israel has had a long-standing policy, which predates Mr. Pollard's involvement with them, of targeting terrorist bases located in Lebanon. Those air strikes are the only exception to this proposition. If the information given by Mr. Pollard had altered the military balance, as Secretary Weinberger contends, Israel surely would have begun hostilities against Syria, in light of that country's provocative behavior in Lebanon.

III. MR. POLLARD'S ACCESS TO CLASSIFIED DOCUMENTS

Mr. Pollard commenced his employment with the Department of Navy in 1979 as an intelligence analyst. He immediately attracted the attention of his superiors because of the depth of his analysis and his enthusiasm. Consequently, Mr. Pollard was given extremely favorable reviews and received several awards and promotions. In 1984, he was assigned to the Anti-Terrorist Alert Center, first as a watch officer and later as a research/analyst. From the beginning of his tenure until his arrest in November of 1985, except for a brief period in 1980, he held clearances up to the TOP SECRET level, which permitted him access to a variety of classified documents.

As stated in the United States' memorandum, analysts in the U.S. intelligence community operate on an honor system, in that the analysts voluntarily limit their access to only those documents which they perceive a need to inspect. Unlike the defense establishment, the intelligence community does not have a structured procedure establishing a "need to know" restricting the access of those possessing security clearances to specific categories of information. The primary reason for the more relaxed procedure in the intelligence community is a need for the analysts and researchers to have a ready exchange of ideas and a general awareness of events in parts of the world other than those for which they are responsible. In the intelligence community, there is an overriding goal that analysis of world events not be made in a vacuum. To that end, Mr. Pollard would, as part of normal procedure, be permitted access to a wide range of classified material.

Not only would Mr. Pollard have access to documents dealing with subjects outside his assigned specialty—the Caribbean—it was assumed, and indeed expected, that he would keep abreast of developments in other areas of the world. As a watch officer, Mr. Pollard was obligated to monitor all incoming information germane to terrorist activities anywhere in the world. Furthermore, Mr. Pollard's superiors came to rely on his expertise in the Middle East, gained through his prior assignments with the Navy and his willingness to take the time to absorb available information, such that he was called upon on many occasions to deliver explanations of the significance of events in the Middle East. Indeed, Mr. Pollard's superiors sent him as the official Navy representative to two high level inter-agency intelligence conferences dealing, in part, with developments in the Middle East. Because of his expertise in matters in that region, it was anticipated by Mr. Pollard and his superiors that he would be assigned to the Middle East desk as soon as a position was available, and that it therefore was imperative that he stay current on Middle East affairs.

In spite of its full awareness of the above, the United States has sought to depict Mr. Pollard as actively ransacking the intelligence libraries to provide information to Israel. Indeed, the United States intended that he have such access. While this distinction does not exonerate Mr. Pollard from the charge to which he has pled guilty, it clarifies that his access to classified documents regarding the Middle East was facilitated knowingly by the U.S. Government and was not the product of his contrivance.

IV. MR. POLLARD'S DECISION TO PROVIDE INFORMATION TO ISRAEL

At the outset, the Court should be aware, and the United States has not disputed, that Mr. Pollard did not join the U.S. intelligence community with the intent of providing information to Israel. Instead, as explained in Mr. Pollard's version of the offense, his decision to become an employee of the U.S. Navy was motivated by a desire to help the United States, to fight communism, and to [have] a meaningful impact on combating terrorism. It was only after several years of frustration over aspects of U.S. policy that Mr. Pollard even began considering an approach to the Israelis. Finally, when events in the Middle East threatened the interests of both the

United States and Israel, and when he felt that the United States was not providing to Israel that which was called for in the intelligence exchange agreements between the two countries, did he make an overture to the Israelis to provide them with that information. While one can scarcely condone the judgment to approach the Israelis and to provide them with such information, Mr. Pollard's motivations were ideological, not mercenary. The corruptive effect of money on his conduct, fully discussed in his statement, came later. In the beginning and for five months thereafter, Mr. Pollard received *no* money for his activity. Moreover, as further testament to the non-mercenary motivation of his conduct, he was in service for six years before he made his fateful decision to help Israel. Lastly, it must be noted that his motives were probed by polygraphy and on this issue he was found to be telling the truth— he acted out of ideology first, not for money.

A. Mr. Pollard's Pro-Israel Viewpoint

Mr. Pollard has explained at length the circumstances of his upbringing and religion which inculcated a sympathy towards the State of Israel and which led him to provide information to it. His Jewish heritage, his trip to Israel, extensive reading of Jewish and Israeli history, and exposure to the attitudes of his family and friends naturally induced a strong pro-Israeli posture. Mr. Pollard's work experience only intensified this feeling towards Israel. As analyst privy to classified information, he became aware of the true danger to Israel from its enemies in the Middle East and thought that the U.S. public underestimated or did not appreciate this danger. More importantly, Mr. Pollard thought that the U.S. intelligence community was deliberately withholding information from Israel that was vital to its security, even though formal intelligence exchange agreements provided that the information be shared with Israel. He learned of the existence of these exchange agreements and their contours from his role as a delegate to several joint U.S.-Israel conferences at which information was exchanged pursuant to the agreements. Mr. Pollard, who had never hidden his feelings towards Israel, on several ocasions challenged the failure of the U.S. to provide certain documents to the Israelis, and demanded an explanation from his superiors. Not only did his superiors refuse to provide any reason for the policy of withholding information, their replies often contained anti-Semitic overtones. On one occasion, when he protested the failure to turn over information regarding Soviet chemical warfare capabilities to the Israeli intelligence counterpart, Mr. Pollard was told that Jews are overly sensitive about gas because of their experiences during World War II.

B. *Frustration over Terrorism*

Concurrent with Mr. Pollard's growing alarm over the threat to Israel's very existence and the United States' reluctance to provide the information necessary to aid Israel was his increasing distress over the threat of terrorism to the United States. Mr. Pollard always has viewed [himself] as being a loyal son of both the United States and Israel. Accordingly, when events like the bombing of the Marine barracks in Beirut occurred, Mr. Pollard felt a rage both that the U.S. intelligence system failed to prevent such a tragedy and also that the United States failed to retaliate, even though it was well aware of the culprits behind the bombing. Because Mr. Pollard questioned the political resolve of the United States to take the actions necessary to combat terrorism effectively, he thought it necessary to do all he could to assist the one country—Israel—that had demonstrated the fortitude to strike at terrorists. The fact that the major terrorist organization in the world, the Palestine Liberation Organization, targets its operations almost exclusively at Israel and the United States, rendered the decision more justifiable in his mind.

V. MR. POLLARD'S LIMITATIONS ON DELIVERY OF INFORMATION

Consistent with Mr. Pollard's motivation in providing information to Israel were the limitations he imposed on the type of documents he would supply. He did not adopt the blind attitude that what was good for Israel was good for the United States; rather, he realized that the interests of Israel and the United States occasionally diverged. Mr. Pollard accordingly insisted, with the concurrence of the Israelis, that he would not divulge information concerning U.S. military or intelligence capabilities, or take any other action deemed to damage the U.S. national security. He provided only information he thought would benefit the defense of Israel, which fell into the following general categories: (1) the weapon systems of Arab countries; (2) the intelligence structures and capabilities of Arab countries; (3) daily message traffic concerning events in the Middle East; (4) analysis of Soviet weapon systems which would probably be delivered to Soviet client states in the Middle East; and (5) analysis of Arab leaders, political intentions and governmental stability.

Restrictions on the type of information which Mr. Pollard supplied are hardly consistent with the United States' depiction of him. One who sells state secrets solely for money is unlikely to anger his benefactors by denying them access to certain documents. Yet, Mr. Pollard flatly refused Eitan's demand

(2½ lines censored out)

On other occasions, Eitan asked for information regarding U.S. intelligence sources in Israel

(3½ lines censored out)

Eitan also demanded documents concerning U.S. knowledge of Israeli arms dealings with other countries, particularly China, and U.S. knowledge of Israeli intelligence efforts in the United States. Each time Mr. Pollard would not provide such documentation or information, despite Eitan's threats of recrimination.

VI. COMPENSATION

A. *The Decision to Accept Compensation*

The predominant theme in the United States' memorandum is that Mr. Pollard's decision to deliver information to the Israelis was motivated solely by the allure of money. Mr. Pollard does not contest that he received compensation for his efforts to provide classified information to the Israelis; in all other aspects the United States memorandum is distortive of the actual sequence of events leading to that compensation.

As correctly pointed out in the United States' memorandum, Mr. Pollard was put in contact with Avi Sella in June, 1984, regarding a desire to aid Israel that Mr. Pollard had professed to a mutual friend. Sella asked that Mr. Pollard provide a sample of the type of information to which he had access. Mr. Pollard did so, without requesting or receiving any remuneration. Shortly thereafter, Mr. Pollard commenced providing documents to the Israelis on a regular basis, again without demanding or receiving compensation. Mr. Pollard and Sella only discussed compensation because Sella stated that standard practice dictated that all "agents" receive compensation for their activities. This policy probably reflected the Israeli's conviction that one who provided information for ideological reasons was less likely to stay the course than one who acted for the money. Indeed, when later Mr. Pollard offered to repay the Israelis for the money given him, his previous handler, Avi Sella, stated that the offer was unacceptable, because Rafi Eitan, the head of the operation, did not like his agents to discover morality.[5]

In the initial discussion between Mr. Pollard and Sella regarding money, a variety of options was explored. Mr. Pollard said that he was considering moving to New York so that his wife could further her career. Sella obviously was concerned because such a move would deprive the Israelis of a source of information; therefore, he offered to provide a job for Mr. Pollard's wife in the Washington area. The problem with such an approach was that it could force Mr. Pollard to involve indirectly his wife in his activities, which neither he nor the Israelis desired. Sella then offered to pay Mr. Pollard a sum which would compensate him for the income lost by his wife by remaining in Washington. Such a proposal was not implemented immediately, and only in November, 1984, did the Israelis and Mr. Pollard discuss and agree upon payments to him of $1500 per month. Accordingly, Mr. Pollard provided information to Israel for five months without receipt of any compensation, and without any reasonable assurance that he would receive any in the future. Obviously, if the Israelis had decided to terminate the operation in November, 1984, Mr. Pollard would have had no recourse against them. His willingness to risk the possibility of arrest for five months without any tangible and immediate financial reward hardly is consistent with the image painted by the United States of him as a cynical mercenary.

Even more importantly, the United States fails to mention that its polygraph operator specifically interrogated Mr. Pollard on his motivations for providing information to Israel. The polygraph operator found no deception when Mr. Pollard stated that he acted primarily for ideological reasons.

B. Mr. Pollard's Spending Habits

Perhaps, in recognition that it cannot dispute the results of the polygraph examination it conducted showing an ideological motivation for Mr. Pollard's actions, the United States focuses on Mr. Pollard's use of the money he received, rather than his desire for it. Again, Mr. Pollard does not challenge receipt of the money, nor the expenditure of it; however, he cannot accept the picture of corruption painted by the United States' memorandum.

Before he received any payments from the Israelis, Mr. Pollard and his wife had established a lifestyle which included almost daily lunches or dinners at restaurants in the Washington area, frequent purchases of clothes and books, and entertainment. On the other hand, he and his wife rented a modest apartment, owned a single, dated nondescript automobile, and were paying off student loans. Mr. Pollard was not massively in debt, however, and he and his wife's spending did not exceed their disposable income. Accordingly, he did not perceive the payments from the Israelis to be rescuing him from financial straits.

In November, 1984, Mr. Pollard and the Israelis agreed that he would be paid $1500 per month, commencing immediately. The Israelis did not give Mr. Pollard any money for his efforts on their behalf for the previous five months. Mr. Pollard received $1500 per month for about nine months, until the Israelis raised the amount to $2500. Contrary to the implication in the United States' memorandum, Mr. Pollard did not demand a raise, but the Israelis offered (and he received) an increase because of the quality of the material being supplied by him. In all, Mr. Pollard received approximately $25,000 in cash payments from the Israelis for the period from November 1984 through November 1985.

The effect of the money given by the Israelis was to upgrade Mr. Pollard's standard of living, not to transform him and his wife into profligate spenders. For example, Mr. Pollard and his wife went to nicer restaurants, selected more expensive clothing, and bought hardback, instead of paperback, books. Also, Mr. Pollard and his wife made trips to friends' weddings and social events that they would have eschewed previously. There is no contention that he or his wife have stashed any money in the United States or abroad or that they used the money for any illicit purpose.

Mr. Pollard and his wife also made two trips to Europe that were sponsored by the Israelis. The United States has delighted in detailing the amount of money spent on those trips, yet the United States overlooks the fact that the trips were required by the Israelis, so that they could meet with Mr. Pollard outside the reach of U.S. law enforcement jurisdiction. When considering the extensive travel involved, the minimum costs associated with the trips would have run into the thousands of dollars. While Mr. Pollard did have luxurious accommodations on many segments of the trip, the Israelis urged that he enjoy himself to the maximum extent possible, particularly since on one trip he and his wife were on their honeymoon. Furthermore, the Israelis requested that Mr. Pollard rent a suite in one hotel in Paris, which cost over $300 per day, so that meetings between them could take place there. When the Israelis found an alternate meeting place, Mr. Pollard immediately moved to a room costing $75 per night. In addition, he and his wife travelled typically on coach fare, especially between the United States and Europe, and stayed overnight at modest establishments on many occasions.

The United States also emphasizes, as part of its characterization of Mr. Pollard as being motivated solely by lucre, that the Israelis promised him that they were putting $30,000 per year into a Swiss bank account in the name of Danny Cohen. While the Israelis showed Mr. Pollard a passport in that name, they never exhibited any proof that the Swiss account actually existed or that they had deposited any money into the account. Furthermore, the Israelis admitted to Mr. Pollard that the account, if it existed, would be accessible by him only on the countersignature of an appropriate Israeli agent. Accordingly, Mr. Pollard had little, if any, expectation of receiving funds from this source, and indeed, never obtained money from the account. Furthermore, the United States has determined that the account was devoid of funds. It is absurd, therefore, for the United States to intimate that the bank account drove Mr. Pollard to further efforts on behalf of the Israelis.

VII. MR. POLLARD AS A RECIDIVIST

In its sentencing memorandum, the United States discusses several other episodes in which Mr. Pollard divulged classified information to other persons allegedly not entitled to access to the information. Mr. Pollard does not contest that he provided information to such persons; however, he does take issue with the version offered by the United States of the circumstances surrounding the delivery of information. It is important for the Court to realize that the United States almost invariably relies on the word of the recipients of the information when discussing the incidents. With good reason, the credibility of those recipients is open to substantial doubt.

In no instance did the recipient of the information voluntarily come forward immediately to disclose Mr. Pollard's conduct to the proper authorities. In a few cases, the recipient, in what is reminiscent of a "race to the courthouse," approached the U.S. investigators after news of Mr. Pollard's arrest became known. These belated "confessions" can be attributed solely to the recipient's fears that Mr. Pollard would disclose the delivery of information and therefore subject them to criminal charges. Those recipients accordingly thought it preferable to provide their version of the incident first. In other cases, the United States learned of the passing of information only after notified of the incident by Mr. Pollard. Only when summoned by the investigators did those persons provide an account of the passing of information.

In spite of the tardiness with which the recipients of information from Mr. Pollard provided U.S. authorities with their version of the transaction, the United States did not see fit to charge any of those individuals with violations of the espionage laws. Even stranger, the United States did not even subject the recipients to a lie detector test to ascertain either the accuracy of their statements or their motives in seeking and receiving information from Mr. Pollard. By contrast, the United States examined Mr. Pollard thoroughly while he was connected to a polygraph and is satisfied with his answers. Nevertheless, the United States insists on providing a description of the incidents which relies primarily on the version given by the recipients of the information, rather than Mr. Pollard's polygraph-tested explanation.

A. Peter Mole

Mole was an officer of the Australian Navy assigned to act as liaison officer with the United States pursuant to an exchange of information agreement. Because Mole was an officer of one of the United States' strongest allies and assigned specifically to receive classified information on behalf of his government, he was permitted to have access to information passing through the Department of Navy Intelligence center. On several occasions, Mr. Pollard was instructed by his superiors to ensure that Mole be given any documents he requested, regardless of the type or secrecy level of the document. Even though many of the documents contained the notation "NOFORN," which forbids dissemination to foreign governments, Mr. Pollard's superiors ordered complete access for Mole, and justified the order by declaring that Mole was considered a U.S. employee. Accordingly, when Mole asked Mr. Pollard for information relating to U.S.-New Zealand affairs, Mr. Pollard saw no impropriety in providing a document responsive to the request. Indeed, investigators later not only acknowledged the extent to which Navy personnel routinely gave Mole access to restricted classified information, but they devoted a lengthy debriefing session to discussing the latent security problem of permitting British, Canadian and Australian liaison officers to have carte blanche in obtaining classified documents.

B. Kurt Lohbeck, Joe Harmon and Laura Caro

Neither Lohbeck, Harmon nor Caro possessed security clearances, and Mr. Pollard does not contend that his divulging of classified information to them was in any way sanctioned by his superiors. Mr. Pollard's actions were not, however, examples of recidivist behavior, but rather reflected an unfortunate desire to impress his friends with the importance of his work and his knowledge of areas of interest to them. Interestingly, the United States has not contended that those individuals who received information from Mr. Pollard passed it on to unfriendly countries or used it in a manner detrimental to the national security. Indeed, the United States' memorandum is devoid of any claims of damage arising from the passing of information to those persons. While this lack of damage does not condone the action, it does justify a more re-strained punishment.[6]

The United States also attempts to assign several sinister motives to what basically was a simple memory lapse. Mr. Pollard truly was unable to remember the details surrounding the disclosure of information to the above individuals. This lack of recall signifies neither a cavalier attitude towards classified information nor a realization that the disclosures were inconsistent with his motivations in passing information to Israel. Instead, Mr. Pollard's temporary memory lapse can be attributed simply to his focus on the aspects of his dealings with the Israelis. Given his overriding desire to provide all information he could give regarding the extent of his activities on behalf of the Israelis, it is not unnatural that he would lose track of unrelated incidents. Furthermore, the United States has not suggested that he was in any way deceitful regarding his answers once he recalled the events on which he was being questioned.

C. *The South African Affair*

While he was still a graduate student, Mr. Pollard struck up an acquaintance with a military attaché at the South African embassy. This relationship, begun at a reception at the South African embassy, continued through correspondence and occasional phone calls. Because Mr. Pollard did not possess a security clearance at this point, the South African's motivation in speaking to him could be attributable to several innocuous factors, including an appreciation of his knowledge of South African affairs, rare among Americans, a desire to promote friendly relations with America, and perhaps less lofty reasons such as an indulgence of his craving for ego gratification.

When Mr. Pollard commenced his employment with the Department of Navy, he thought it opportune to utilize his contacts with the South Africans. At that time, relations between South Africa and the United States were strained, and intelligence exchanges severed, because of the expulsion of the U.S. military attaché from South Africa for espionage activities. Because the absence of information from South Africa left a hole in the U.S. intelligence gathering network, Mr. Pollard thought it imperative to establish a link with the South Africans. Before making any overtures to the South Africans, he first obtained the consent of his superiors.

(1 page censored out)

VII. MR. POLLARD'S POST-ARREST CONDUCT

The United States' description of the events which took place from November 18, 1985, through Mr. Pollard's arrest on November 21 are correct. Mr. Pollard deliberately misled U.S. investigators as to the nature of his activities on behalf of Israel, in an effort to permit his Israeli handlers to escape. Mr. Pollard does not ask the Court to excuse this conduct, but to recognize that this was the result of his desire to reciprocate the assurances of his handlers, that in a crisis they would assist him, by protecting them. Such gullibility is understandable when one appreciates the ideological motivation for Mr. Pollard's conduct. Indeed, this ideological motivation supplanted his instinct for personal survival during those critical days and hours prior to his arrest. In that time, Mr. Pollard never made a break for it until he had confessed several times to the act of espionage (albeit without identifying his handlers); he telegraphed every move to his interrogators; he consented to warrantless searches of his apartment; and he drove amateurishly to a promised haven that never existed at the Israeli embassy. Of course, when Mr. Pollard was finally arrested he never attempted to bargain his situation for that of his handlers. If his passing of information to the Israelis had been driven solely by money, as the Government persists was the case, Mr. Pollard most assuredly would have tried, upon his arrest, to obtain a bargain in return for identification of his confederates. This did not happen. This is not a condonation of conduct, but rather an explanation that serves to underscore the profound ideological commitment of Mr. Pollard to his conduct and, concomitantly, the utter naiveté he demonstrated at a time when his life was collapsing around him.

A. Mr. Pollard's Cooperation with the Government and its Value

The Court should also weigh heavily the cooperation extended by Mr. Pollard beginning three months after his arrest and well before a plea agreement was executed. Without the promise of any le-

niency by the United States, except its commitment not to ask for a
life sentence or a specific term of years but only for a "substantial"
period of incarceration, Mr. Pollard began providing full details of
his activities on behalf of the Israelis. The ensuing debriefings
consumed several hundred hours, during which Mr. Pollard provided information to his U.S. interrogators on the following subjects:

(3 pages censored out)

Mr. Pollard is continuing to assist in the ongoing criminal investigation through interviews and grand jury testimony. For
example, he has appeared before the grand jury investigating the
role of Avi Sella twice in the last month to detail Sella's direct
request and receipt of classified information from him.

Because of Mr. Pollard's candor in describing the extent of the
information passed to Israel, the United States has been able to
gauge more accurately the extent of any damage caused by Mr.
Pollard's actions and to take effective countermeasures. In addition,
his forthrightness has enabled the United States to confront the
Israelis regarding the truth of the statements they submitted to the
U.S. investigators.

Mr. Pollard's cooperation also has extended beyond identifying
the scope of his activities for Israel. A prevalent concern in the U.S.
intelligence community was how he could pass documents to the
Israelis for eighteen months without detection. Mr. Pollard not only
supplied details of his ability to circumvent security measures at
his workplace and the intelligence libraries, he also provided advice
on how best to rectify those holes in the security net. For instance,
Mr. Pollard explained how modems, which permit communication
with a computer by phone, represent a severe security problem
since the high speed transmissions could be intercepted by enemy
agents acting outside secure facilities, who could quickly access
massive amounts of classified information. He also discussed how
secretion of a single floppy disk from a secured area could be as
damaging as the removal of hundreds of classified documents. In
addition, he advised investigators that the State Department Intelligence and Research Bureau is probably the optimum location for
an enemy spy, since analysts at the Bureau routinely receive hun-

dreds of intelligence reports weekly as part of their duty of summarizing such reports for reading by the Secretary of State.

Several times during his marathon debriefings, officials of various intelligence agencies commented favorably on the ideas put forward by Mr. Pollard. Others assured him that his recommendations had been implemented.

Mr. Pollard's cooperation with investigators also was so impressive and his previous employment evaluation so favorable that his questioners began to take the interrogation beyond the realm of his activities for Israel. For example, after Mr. Pollard's debriefing had terminated, he was brought back from prison to give various intelligence officers a briefing

(line censored out)

The United States concedes that Mr. Pollard was "candid and informative in describing his wrongdoing," and that the investigation of the Israeli involvement in the matter could not have progressed as far as it did without his assistance. The Government's description of Mr. Pollard's cooperation, however, is lame in the extreme. Without the benefit of the detail which is supplied above, there is no way the Court could possibly discern the level, depth and value of Mr. Pollard's cooperation. By failing to give Mr. Pollard proper credit for his cooperation, the Government has not honored its part of the plea bargain. Instead, it offers the shrillness of an overstated argument to support its claim for a substantial sentence. This is not fair. If the Government wishes to attack Mr. Pollard's honesty, it is free to do so, but not at the expense of failing to speak as candidly and openly about his valuable cooperation as it has about his criminal conduct.

B. Mr. Pollard's Conduct and Treatment in Prison

In addition to cooperating extensively with the prosecutors and officials of the U.S. intelligence community, Mr. Pollard has displayed a compliant attitude towards prison and jail officials. Mr. Pollard has been a model prisoner, even in the face of disturbing patterns of harassment. Since his arrest, Mr. Pollard has been kept in administrative detention, resulting in isolation from others, and curtailed exercise, phone, and visitation privileges. This detention has not been imposed because of any perception that Mr. Pollard is a discipline problem, but rather because of a concern that other prisoners would cause harm to him. Because of the nature of the offense to which Mr. Pollard has pled guilty and because of his Jewish background, prison officials fear that he is a target for several prison groups. In particular, Mr. Pollard has received threats from the Aryan Brotherhood, which is renowned in the prison system for its anti-Semitism.[8] In spite of this, Mr. Pollard has requested on numerous occasions that he be put in less restrictive surroundings so that he may enjoy the same privileges as other prisoners, even though such a move would expose him to greater danger.

An added burden for Mr. Pollard is that several of his guards have displayed a bigotry similar to that of the Aryan Brotherhood, as revealed not only in derogatory remarks to him but also in unusually harsh treatment. For example, on one occasion, Mr. Pollard's jailors at Petersburg, Virginia, told him he was going home to Israel, then chained him by the throat, waist and feet, and placed him in a van for transport to the federal prison at Lewisburg, Pennsylvania. At the beginning of the lengthy trip, the jailors delighted in taunting Mr. Pollard with anti-Semitic remarks. At Lewisburg, Mr. Pollard was treated erroneously as a discipline problem, with further restrictions on visitation and phone privileges. In addition, during the brief visit that prison officials permitted him to have with his wife, his hands were cuffed and placed in a box which was designed to tighten the handcuffs if he attempted to move his hands. Excessive movement of the hands in the box could result in a broken wrist. Even though intercession by the U.S. Attorney's Office provided a reprieve from this treatment, its pervasiveness, grounded in bigotry and the expectable hostility of our society to spies, combine to make Mr. Pollard's incarceration especially brutal.

C. Mr. Pollard's Physical, Emotional, and Judgmental Deterioration

It is not surprising that any person incarcerated for more than a year will suffer breakdowns in health, both physical and mental. It is also the case that his judgment will not always be as acute as in other less stressful circumstances.

In Mr. Pollard's case, this deterioration has been rapid and profound. It is compounded by the fact that his wife, Anne Henderson-Pollard, has, to his way of thinking, suffered even more than he—and he has been able to do nothing about it. He has witnessed her decline in health, as evidenced by the loss of more than sixty pounds, an excruciatingly painful surgery, numerous endoscopic examinations, extreme dependence on pain medication, and a marked deterioration in her morale. She has been subjected to an onslaught of media people, each of whom carry a special message of why it is important for her and/or her husband to speak to them.

Both Mr. and Mrs. Pollard have lapsed in this regard and, against better judgment and advice, have spoken to the press. Hopefully, this will be seen as an aberration, nothing more. Rather, these are the acts of a person who, notwithstanding valuable cooperation, has been held up to vilification and scorn, whose motives, although verified as ideological, have been condemned as mercenary, whose lifestyle, although demonstrably modest, has been described as profligate, and whose personal integrity, although tested severely during his cooperation, has been impugned. It is reflective of the desperation that grips these people in this, the lowest moment of their lives.

Mr. Pollard's incarceration and its special debilitating features are discussed above. Here we wish the Court to understand the special torture this situation represents. A family is destroyed, a marital relationship severed, the daily threat of bodily harm, and the specter of long-term imprisonment and isolation all coalesce in this case with a force far greater than usual. This is because no degree of intellectualizing can correct the crushing realization that Mr. Pollard may have no life before him and this notwithstanding that he feels he has betrayed no one, and never intended or did harm to the United States.

IX. POSSIBILITY OF PAROLE

A factor which the Court should consider in imposing sentence is the likelihood of whether Mr. Pollard will be paroled at any time during his incarceration. In this instance, given the nature of the offense, parole is highly improbable. The sentencing guidelines call for any person convicted of espionage to serve *at least* 100 months, or eight and one-third years in prison, before he is even considered for release on parole. See 28 CFR Pp 2.20. Furthermore, there is no guarantee that the Parole Board would release Mr. Pollard on parole even after he served 100 months, especially since, to the best of our knowledge, the Parole Board has not paroled one person convicted of espionage laws in the past ten years. The Court accordingly could reasonably presume that Mr. Pollard will have to serve fully any sentence imposed by it, less any reduction for good behavior. Applying this measure, in any sentence in excess of five years, Mr. Pollard will likely serve fully two-thirds of the high end of any sentence imposed by the Court. See 18 U.S.C. 4206(d).

CONCLUSION

Since the codes of Hammurabi, the laws have evolved to a simple but profound proposition, *viz.* that punishment should fit the crime. Enlightened sentencing principles in today's jurisprudence look beyond the sensational aspects that often accompany the establishment of guilt in favor of measuring the severity of the offense. This is especially true where the defendant has pled guilty to the crime.

In this case, notwithstanding its sensational features, where an enormous volume of information was transmitted improperly, it was done without the intent to, and without the result of, damaging the nation's security. This case is lacking the essential ingredient that would make this a heinous crime: the beneficiary was not, and is not, the enemy, but one of our closest friends. By this, we do not argue that what Mr. Pollard did was right, or that it does not merit punishment. However, the punishment must be appropriate to the actual severity of his criminal conduct. Applying that measure, no harm has come to the country. Accordingly, Mr. Pollard's sentence ought to reflect this indisputable fact.

FOOTNOTES

(1) The Weinberger affidavit must be recognized as not having been written by the Secretary of Defense. In the true spirit of overkill that characterizes the Government's assessment of damage in this case, the attempt to make more out of what is the real injury to the national security is demonstrated by this technique of having the Secretary

sign the affidavit rather than the true author(s). In a pending espionage prosecution in the Eastern District of Virginia, in which the undersigned are also counsel, the damage assessments in that case were *not* signed by the Secretary of Defense. The point is noted here because this Court should not be bulldozed into not considering a challenge to a document just because it was signed by a cabinet secretary.

(2) There is nothing in the damage assessment that speaks of damage to our national security in terms of our position vis-a-vis the Soviets. The first occasion where such a claim arises is in the Government's opposition to Mr. Pollard's recently-denied Motion for Production of Evidence Favorable to the Accused. Since the allegation was made and because of its incendiary nature, it is important to focus on it in order to point out that there is simply no basis in the evidence for it.

The only reference in the damage assessment to the Soviet Union regards the danger of a Soviet mole in Israeli intelligence. That issue is treated *infra*.

Unless the government is sandbagging everyone by bringing in such proof in "rebuttal," the record as it stands merely speculates, without any proof, that somehow our national security vis-a-vis Russia potentially has been damaged. To state this, without more, is overkill and exploitive of a situation in which the Government holds every advantage and the defendant has no opportunity for rebuttal.

(3) Secretary Weinberger also laments the possibility that Mr. Pollard could have been a victim of a "false flag" operation. A "false flag" is a situation where the offender is duped into believing that he is giving information to a perfectly benevolent recipient when in fact the ultimate recipient is the enemy. It is true that a "false flag" can operate in every espionage; however it should also be factored into the question of punishment that there was *no* "false flag" here. Again, we reiterate that the Court should assess the actual damage, not what it could have done. All the indicia of the "flag" pointed squarely to Israel and nothing in Mr. Pollard's experience belied that. Thus, Mr. Pollard knew then Colonel—now General—Avi Sella to be an Israeli military hero who led the bombing raid on the Iraqi nuclear reactor site in 1981. While residing in New York, Sella's wife was nationally active in the Anti-Defamation League. In addition, Sella provided Mr. Pollard the entree to Yossi Yagur and Irit Erb, who became his long-term handlers. Most significantly, he met at length with Rafael Eitan, the ultimate controller of the operation, the man who "captured" Adolf Eichmann. Throughout the course of his operation, Mr. Pollard questioned all of these individuals at length to satisfy his curiosity, and to establish their bona fides. Even the best trained agents could not have known the details or events on which these individuals were quizzed. The specter of a "false flag" was, in reality, therefore, non-existent.

(4) When questioned by reporters on how the Israelis were certain that they were striking at PLO members, rather than Tunisian civilians, President Reagan replied, "I have always had great faith in their intelligence." *Id.*

(5) The United States attacks the veracity of Mr. Pollard's offer to reimburse the Israelis for the monies given him by claiming that he initially told authorities that he had conveyed his offer to Yossi Yagur by letter, but that he retracted the statement when asked to submit to a polygraph examination. The actual sequence of events was that Mr. Pollard told authorities that he had asked Irit Erb to write Yagur to offer repayment of the monies. The authorities became confused when Mr. Pollard said that he had not orally told Yossi of his offer and they assumed that he meant he had written a letter to Yossi instead of having Irit prepare the letter. This confusion was natural, since Mr. Pollard had written Yossi directly regarding shipments of arms to the Iranians to defend Kharg Island. When the subject came up during the course of an extensive polygraph examination, Mr. Pollard clarified the authorities' confusion. It is unfortunate that the Government attempts to accentuate this confusion, especially since it does not otherwise challenge the truthfulness of Mr. Pollard's offer of repayment to the Israelis.

(6) In Lohbeck's case, little damage could have occurred. As a recognized liaison to the Mujaheddin, Lohbeck not only had access to several key U.S. officials, including Robert

McFarlane, but also to intelligence reports. On several occasions, Lohbeck showed Mr. Pollard classified documents with security caveats so high that he was unaware they existed. Mr. Pollard therefore thought it acceptable to provide Lohbeck with relatively less sensitive information concerning events in Afghanistan. Mr. Pollard provided such information in an effort to assist Lohbeck in crossing the border into Afghanistan and to further arms sales that they were attempting to arrange. For unexplained reasons, investigators did not seek details regarding Lohbeck's ties with U.S. officials or the documents shown Mr. Pollard by Lohbeck; indeed, on two occasions an investigator involved in Mr. Pollard's debriefing specifically instructed him to cut short narratives concerning these topics.

(7) Censored out

(8) On three separate occasions, Mr. Pollard received warnings from other inmates that the Aryan Brotherhood has targeted him for assassination. Prison officials, respectful of the justifiable pride which the Brotherhood takes in fulfilling its threats, has attempted to monitor known Brotherhood members in the prison. According to inmates, however, the Brotherhood has promised to put a "sleeper," or a clandestine member of the group, in the prison to carry out its avowed execution.

LETTER TO SENTENCING JUDGE FROM BERNARD HENDERSON ON BEHALF OF ANNE HENDERSON POLLARD

Falls Church, VA
January 14, 1987

Chief Judge Aubrey E.
    Robinson, Jr.
United States District Court
for the District of Columbia
Washington, D.C. 20001

Dear Judge Robinson:

I am writing on behalf of my daughter, Anne Pollard, to plea for leniency to the letter of the law and, more importantly, for justice to the overriding human and moral values involved.

I bear a heavy responsibility in urging her to plead guilty to the two charges at a time when she felt she had done nothing to hurt anyone. It took time for her to understand that, under the letter of the law, it is a crime for her, or anyone else not authorized, to possess classified documents, despite the fact that she never reveled [sic] any such information and that trying to help someone you love in his hour of need can also be a crime.

Despite her intelligence and industriousness, Anne has always been very much a romantic. She has an enormous capacity for love, and in that sense, I have been very fortunate having such a wonderful daughter.

I have watched her progress in a field which has many practitioners, but few with genuine talent. She has that talent, and in a relatively short period of time achieved results worthy of professionals decades beyond her in years.

My judgment of that is based on many years of top level experience in engineering, journalism, publishing and public relations.

In publishing, I progressed from assistant editor to chief editor and publisher for newspapers and trade magazines. In public relations, I handled major clients for Hill & Knowlton and later was in charge of public relations for a division of Gulf & Western, the Teamsters Union, a division of AMAX and Quaker State Oil Refining Corporation. I have written thousands of articles and speeches, including two for President Ford. I am well-known in the Washington public relations and press community, as well as in other areas.

During the past several years, I have advised Anne constantly about her work and professional development. Last year, I encouraged her to establish her own business and worked closely with her as she managed to become Washington director for CommCore, a public relations firm with an established list of blue-chip clients, as well as Publicity Director for the National Independence Day Parade and Festival. And believe me, the nation would have enjoyed a far better celebration had she been allowed to continue.

She planned and wrote reams of public relations proposals for these organizations and was well on her way to establishing herself in Washington. During that time, we often spoke daily by phone and I was aware of the enormous time and effort she put into her work.

That's why I was so flabbergasted, after her husband's arrest, that anyone would think she had even the time, let alone the interest, to be directly involved in espionage.

That's why I was so shocked to see her thrown into isolated detention on a street arrest. In my judgment, the severity of that detention, outside of physical torture, ranks with the POW camps in Korea and Viet Nam. I watched her, caged and shackled, lose 50 pounds as the first strands of her hair began turning gray. As a prison official explained, "Hardened criminals usually crack in three weeks."

She endured it for 95 days.

She was certainly no hardened criminal. In fact, we had reluctantly agreed to the isolation to try to protect her from the world of hardened criminals, prostitutes and drug addicts. As a very small 25-year-old, she would be relatively unprotected from mental and physical abuse they could impose. Of course we had not reckoned with her early inability to obtain medication and medical treatment, and the very serious threat to her life that it imposed [sic]. She was near death upon her release.

Nor had we reckoned with the additional detention pressures: the prohibition of reading material; the lack of exercise; the prohibition of anyone speaking to her and the punishment that befell anyone who did; the almost total restriction from using the phone; the delay or loss of her mail, both incoming and outgoing; the lack of adequate lighting or of toilet facilities; the almost unbearable 100 degree, high humidity heat; the constant glare of lights but no sunshine; and the prohibition from leaving her tiny cockroach and rat infested cell for more than a few half-hour periods each day.

Today I am grateful for the many prison officials and personnel who, against orders, went out of their way to lesson the severity by providing her with both medication and other items that helped make her existence somewhat bearable. Virtually to a person, they agreed she did not belong there. Many told me of their relief and happiness about her release.

Of course, much of her suffering was from lack of adequate medical attention. Anne has suffered abdominal pains for years and takes a great deal of medication to keep a bezoar and ulcers under control, as well as severe, uncontrolled biliary problems.

There is no question that the tortuous detention she underwent exacerbated her condition, making necessary weeks of hospitalization and major surgery at various times following her release. It is possible she may never fully recover.

Ultimately the prosecutors admitted that most of the stories they had cited to plea for her detention were not true, and finally they agreed in writing in their plea bargain agreement that she never engaged in espionage and never passed documents to a foreign national.

In commenting on Anne's sense of values and why she would attempt to help her husband when it would have been more expedient to turn on him and avoid any charges as others have done, I can only say that such a decision would be very difficult for me as well. It has nothing to do with being Jewish (I am not). It's partly a question of legality versus morality. Does a wife's duty to her loved ones transcend her duty to the state? I hope I never face that decision, but it is a given that one must always do everything in their [sic] power to help their [sic] loved ones in their [sic] hour of request.

Anne and I have discussed that decision, which to her was never a conscious one because the series of events leading to the charges were basically outside of her control, and what seemed morally right to her at the time seemed necessary and only later appeared legally wrong.

Anne's values are typical middle-class professional. When she was two years old, we moved from New York to a new home in a suburban New Jersey community. She excelled in school and participated in many school and community activities. She took many part time jobs to earn spending money and was frugal in her habits.

When she was 17, I separated from my wife and moved to Washington, D.C. as press secretary to the Teamsters Union at the request of Bob Gray, whose firm recently merged with Hill & Knowlton.

During the following year, Anne and my son, John, came to Washington to live with me. Anne completed high school at Emerson, the city's oldest private school, completing a year's studies in three months, with final grades ranging from 93 to 100. She received numerous letters of commendation for her outstanding school achievements. I subsequently obtained a divorce in Washington at great expense and loss of all savings and equity, with the result that I had no funds for her college education.

With Anne's industriousness and intelligence, she obtained reasonable jobs, far exceeding her "educational" levels by obtaining positions only granted to those with college degrees. Thereafter, she decided to share an apartment with friends, and soon enrolled as a full-time evening student in college. She had the independence and ability to establish her own life and career. Further, she paid her college expenses solely, without any college or financial support.

In addition, she provided her brother with a home after my divorce when the court denied me custody and positive guidance for his education until he rejoined me later. In addition to providing him with a loving and supporting environment, she supported him financially. She acted as his best friend, confidant, sibling and parent. She is a very giving person, providing friends with shelter when they needed it and recommendations to help them with their housing and careers.

Anne is truly that type of person—totally unselfish, totally moral, probably as close to a truly good, decent human being as you are likely to come across. I am confident that the information collected for you overwhelmingly attests to her character. She is exceedingly moral and law abiding.

I find it difficult to comment on any problems Anne had in

growing up, because she really didn't have any. She was a very obedient child whose behavior was corrected merely by expressions of disapproval. She never got into trouble, and never gave us serious problems even during the period preceding our separation.

That's why it is very difficult for me to understand those who seek to punish her further. I can understand the desires of a victim of a crime to seek punishment for the perpetrator. But Anne has no victim. I can understand the need of the nation to protect its secrets. But Anne gave no secrets, let alone knew any.

If punishment is designed to fit the crime, I can only plea [sic] that her punishment so far exceeds her mistakes. In addition to her isolation detention, she will have been under virtual house arrest for a year by the time of sentencing. She has been required to report to the pretrial services agency every week and has endured numerous other restrictions on her lifestyle. She has been slandered and vilified by the press as a spy and will forever bear the stigma.

Further imprisonment would subject her to life with a criminal element that she has so far mostly avoided—and would benefit neither her nor society.

On the other hand, if she can get on with her life and career, she promises solid contributions to society. Her working life has only just begun, and she has managed to resume it with new employers. It would be a tragedy to reinterrupt it at this point with a sentence that would be of no use to anyone.

Very sincerely yours,

Bernard R. Henderson

ANNE HENDERSON POLLARD'S MEMORANDUM TO THE COURT

I. INTRODUCTION

Anne Henderson Pollard was arrested on November 22, 1985, after a search revealed classified documents in a suitcase that she had asked friends to retrieve and bring to her. Her husband, Jonathan Jay Pollard, had been arrested the previous day and was subsequently charged with transferring classified documents to Israeli nationals. Mrs. Pollard does not deny that she engaged in the acts that led to her arrest. In fact, she has knowingly and voluntarily pleaded guilty before this Court to a two-count information, which details the facts giving rise to the charges. Contrary to the government's assertions, however, those facts do not support the inference that Mrs. Pollard was engaged in a willful, calculated pattern of behavior over a period of years. Rather, the facts, stripped of the high gloss the government has attempted to put on them, show two instances of misjudgment, born out of acceptance of her husband's faits accomplis and her loyalty and love for him.

As a result of her misjudgment, Mrs. Pollard undeniable [sic] committed two criminal offenses, for which she will stand before the Court for sentencing. That sentence should be a fair and lenient one. While the complete facts outlined in this memorandum do not excuse Mrs. Pollard's behavior, they demonstrate that she was placed in a situation in which any of us might have struggled to make the right decisions. Recognizing that Mrs. Pollard made the wrong decisions, she has already more than suffered for the consequences of her actions. The best course now, for both her and the criminal justice system, is for Mrs. Pollard to be allowed to continue to rebuild her life as a productive member of society. Her further incarceration serves no useful purpose and would be detrimental to her health. Therefore we respectfully recommend that the court suspend the execution of any period of incarceration and place Mrs. Pollard on probation for a period of time.

II. BACKGROUND

A. *Family Background*

Mrs. Pollard was born May 1, 1960 in Brooklyn, New York, the first of two children of Bernard and Elaine Henderson. The family lived in Brooklyn for three years, and then moved to a house in Rockaway, New Jersey that remained their principal residence for the next 13 years. During that time, Mr. Henderson switched his career from geological engineering to public relations.

Mrs. Pollard attended public school in Rockaway until she was 16. She excelled both at academics and numerous extra-curricular activities, including art, music and drama groups. In addition, Mrs. Pollard participated in United Synagogue Youth programs as well as other community groups. Throughout her teens, and as early as age eleven, Mrs. Pollard took various babysitting jobs and assumed a large share of the responsibility for caring for her brother, John, who was six years her junior.

In 1976, the family moved to Bethlehem, Pennsylvania, where her father took a new job. Mrs. Pollard adjusted to the Bethlehem community but found herself suddenly in a distinct minority as a Jew.

In 1977, Bernard and Elaine Henderson separated and were subsequently divorced. Mrs. Pollard sought and obtained a variety of part-time jobs, working at several fast-food restaurants and a clothing store. She also continued to care for her younger brother.

In the spring of 1978, Bernard Henderson left Bethlehem to take a job as press secretary for the Teamsters Union in Washington, D.C. John Henderson finished the school year in Pennsylvania and moved to Washington to live with his father; Mrs. Pollard worked through the summer in Bethlehem and then followed.

Mrs. Pollard entered an accelerated course at Emerson Preparatory School in Washington, earned excellent grades, and graduated in January of 1979. She was accepted at American University but was unable to afford college. Mrs. Pollard took the disappointment in stride and enrolled in Georgetown Secretarial School. By May of 1979, she was working in a secretarial position at the American Institute of Architects ("AIA") and sharing a house with a girlfriend who also worked at AIA.

B. Career

From 1979 through 1985, Mrs. Pollard achieved considerable success in establishing a public relations career. Lacking a college degree in her field, she nevertheless gained expertise on the job, convincing her superiors to give her increasing responsibilities. Thus, she advanced from secretarial positions to editorial and press relations jobs, maintaining a commendably stable employment record in the process. Mrs. Pollard also augmented her experience with university night courses and with occasional consultations with her father for professional advice.

In September of 1979, Mrs. Pollard left AIA for a new job at the Chemical Specialties Manufacturers Association, where she worked for the next two and a quarter years. Her first position there was as the secretary to the Convention and Meeting Management Department. Her duties consisted primarily of taking care of the details of running large meetings, seminars, workshops, and Congressional receptions. She scheduled speakers, organized parties, handled registration, and helped plan the agenda for the meetings. In March of 1981, her department was given the additional responsibility of handling member services, including the solicitation of new members. Although her job title did not formally change, Mrs. Pollard was responsible for helping to develop packages of brochures and other promotional materials used to solicit corporations as new members of the organization. Thus, she began to move closer to her chosen field of public relations.

At the same time, Mrs. Pollard began taking college courses at night at the University of Maryland, pursuing a degree course in radio and television, film and journalism. She enrolled in approximately two courses per semester, initially focusing on courses in public relations techniques.

In January of 1982, Mrs. Pollard became an administrative assistant in the public affairs office of the National Rifle Association ("NRA"). Initially, she organized meetings and trade shows sponsored by the NRA. Soon, however, Mrs. Pollard was given the added responsibility to write an lengthy press guide for the American Shooting Team, explaining the various shooting events and presenting biographies of the team members. Thereafter, having demonstrated her writing ability, she began to write press releases on all of the non-legislative areas of the NRA's activities, including hunting, sports, and safety education. She wrote brochures and additional promotional material, as well as articles for a biweekly tabloid published by her division, entitled *Reports from Washington*.

During the summers of 1982, 1983, and 1984, Mrs. Pollard acted as the press director for the "National Matches" shooting event held for two months at Camp Perry, Ohio. For the two months each summer that she spent in Ohio, she dealt daily with media coverage of the event as well as member relations and education.

In addition to her many other responsibilities, Mrs. Pollard took on the task of running a film library program, marketing and promoting approximately 20 NRA films to schools. She put in long hours, working most evenings and weekends, to keep up with significant amounts of writing as well as marketing, promotion, and press relations work. Despite her supervisor's constant attempts to secure a higher status for Mrs. Pollard to reflect her significant contributions to the job, Mrs. Pollard achieved a formal change in her title only in 1985, when she was finally designated a public relations assistant.

Mrs. Pollard continued to supplement her work experience by outside studies. In addition to the college courses she was taking at night and on weekends, Mrs. Pollard enrolled in several specialized professional courses as well.

By the spring of 1985, Mrs. Pollard's competence and confidence had increased significantly. She had been working in the public relations field for over five years and had acquired a wide range of experience. She determined then that she was ready to strike out on her own as a public relations consultant. Consequently, in July of 1985, Mrs. Pollard left her job at the NRA, after working there for three and a half years.

Mrs. Pollard had learned that one of her father's former public relations colleagues from Hill & Knowlton, Karen Berg, was starting a new public relations firm in New York and had arranged to meet with her. As a result, Ms. Berg hired Mrs. Pollard as the director of the Washington office of the new firm, CommCore. Mrs. Pollard's job was to attract Washington clients to the new firm, working on a freelance commission basis on her own schedule. One of her first new accounts was the promotion of the National Independence Day Parade in Washington, D.C.

That fall, Mrs. Pollard strengthened her relationship with

CommCore. In addition to obtaining clients for CommCore in Washington on a commission basis, she was retained by the firm to provide media training to various corporate clients. For example, she participated in one media training seminar in September of 1985 with Campbell Soup Company and was scheduled to lead a seminar on November 25, 1985 in New Brunswick, New Jersey, for AT&T. Because of her arrest on November 22, 1985, however, she could not attend that seminar.

C. *Jonathan Pollard*

In the summer of 1981, Mrs. Pollard moved into a house with two other young women on Capitol Hill. Through a friend of one of her roommates, Mrs. Pollard met Mr. Pollard. Mrs. Pollard felt like she had made an instant best friend in Mr. Pollard; he later claimed to her to have fallen in love with her at their first meeting.

Mrs. Pollard found Mr. Pollard to be an extremely bright and well-read man who could discuss world affairs and history articulately. She was intrigued by the sophistication and intellectualism she observed in him; yet, he was also a warm, sensitive person, full of humor and lacking the hard edges that would have made his intelligence intimidating. For his part, Mr. Pollard found that Mrs. Pollard shared his love of discoursing on world history and current events and that she shared many of his beliefs as well. He quickly discovered she was someone whom he could love and trust, with no pretenses necessary. By November of 1981, the two had become an inseparable couple. They came to depend on each other, each fulfilling the needs of the other.

In June of 1982, when her lease expired, Mrs. Pollard moved into Mr. Pollard's apartment in Arlington, Virginia. By then, she had already met his parents, who visited Washington, D.C. frequently. Mrs. Pollard was very pleased to discover how quickly she and the Pollards became good friends. She developed a close relationship with the Pollards and spoke with them by telephone almost daily.

Mr. Pollard frequently spoke with Mrs. Pollard about his deep concern about terrorists threats to Israel and was very upset at reading newspaper accounts of bombings, hijackings and other terrorist activities. Mr. Pollard felt strongly that the United States could do more to combat terrorism in the world in general and to assist Israel in particular, and he often voiced his concerns in discussions with Mrs. Pollard and with groups of friends. For her part, Mrs. Pollard shared his anti-Communist, pro-American views and felt compassion for those in Israel and elsewhere who are victimized by terrorism.

In the spring of 1984, Mr. Pollard reiterated that he wanted to help the Israelis, perhaps by providing them with his technical expertise. He then informed Mrs. Pollard that a friend of his from New York City had arranged for Mr. Pollard to meet with an individual who might be able to direct Mr. Pollard in his endeavor. Later, she learned that the individual was an Israeli Air Force official, Colonel Aviem Sella, who was studying at that time toward a graduate degree at New York University.

By the summer of 1984, Mrs. Pollard and Mr. Pollard had settled into a routine. Mrs. Pollard was working long hours doing promotional work for events of the NRA; Mr. Pollard had been promoted at his job at the Naval Support Center. They met virtually every day for lunch and, after work each evening, they would enjoy dinner together at a local restaurant. The couple was living in a $750-per-month, two-bedroom apartment at 1733 20th Street, N.W., near Dupont Circle, where they had moved in December of 1982. Between them, they were earning over $50,000, enough to pay for their essential needs[2] and to indulge their love of dining out, without leaving anything for savings.

Mrs. Pollard first met Colonel Sella later that summer when he and his wife joined the Pollards for dinner. The dinner was purely social; there was no discussion in Mrs. Pollard's presence of a transfer of classified documents by Mr. Pollard to the Israelis. Rather, Colonel Sella introduced himself as an old acquaintance of Mr. Pollard's and a potential business contact. Colonel Sella had previously instructed Mr. Pollard that Mrs. Pollard was not to be informed of their activities.

It was not until later that fall that Mrs. Pollard became aware that Mr. Pollard was actually transferring classified documents from his office to Israeli representatives. Mrs. Pollard learned this when she discovered that Mr. Pollard was bringing the documents home to their apartment. In response to the concerns she voiced to Mr. Pollard about his activities and about the presence of the documents in the apartment, Mr. Pollard told Mrs. Pollard that none of the documents contained information about the United States. He assured her that he was providing a great service to Israel and helping to combat terrorism, while, at the same time, doing no harm to the security of the United States.

In November 1984, the Israelis asked Mr. Pollard to travel to Paris, where Mr. Pollard was to meet a new "handler," Joseph "Yossi" Yagur. They told him to bring Mrs. Pollard with them, but instructed him to tell her that a fictitious rich uncle, Joe Fisher, was financing the trip. Further, since she had already met the Sellas, she would not think it odd to meet them in Paris and to socialize together.[3] After Paris, the couple traveled to other parts of Europe.

The expenses paid of the European trip represented the first money Mr. Pollard had received from the Israelis. Mr. Pollard had not been motivated by any thought of financial reward; rather, he had volunteered out of the urgent need he felt to help Israel. Following his return to the United States, however, Mr. Pollard agreed, at the Israeli insistence, to accept $1,500 per month as payment for his services.

After the November 1984 trip to Europe, Mr. Pollard began to supply Mr. Yagur with documents. Mr. Pollard brought the documents home in a briefcase supplied by Mr. Yagur, which he subsequently used to transport the documents to the Northwest D.C. apartment of Irit Erb, an employee of the Israeli embassy. There, he met with Mr. Yagur, while Ms. Erb photocopied the documents for Mr. Yagur to take with him. Later, Mr. Pollard began bringing documents to Ms. Erb in between his meetings with Mr. Yagur, leaving the briefcase of documents for her to copy over the weekend.[4]

By the summer of 1985, the Israelis had increased their monthly payments to Mr. Pollard to $2,500 per month. Soon thereafter, Mr. Pollard's handlers requested that he make a trip to Israel. The Israelis asked that he bring his fiancee, Mrs. Pollard, and financed the Pollards' travel in Europe as part of the trip. Mrs. Pollard and Mr. Pollard decided to be married in Italy and to regard the trip as a honeymoon.

Mr. Pollard and Mrs. Pollard left in mid-July of 1985, traveling directly to Israel as their first stop. Once again, Mr. Pollard met with Mr. Yagur, Colonel Sella, a man known only as "Uzi," and

Rafael Eitan, the senior Israeli official in charge of the operation, while Mrs. Pollard went sightseeing with Mrs. Yagur. On several evenings, the couples dined together, but no "business" was ever discussed. After one and a half weeks in Israel, the Pollards travelled to Europe before returning to Washington. They were married in Venice on August 9, 1985 in a civil ceremony.

After their honeymoon trip, Mr. Pollard continued to provide the Israelis with classified information. Some of his co-workers apparently became increasingly suspicious, however, as they noticed that he was removing large numbers of classified documents from depository libraries. Such suspicions ultimately led to the investigation and arrest of Mr. Pollard that fall.

III. THE OFFENSES

A. COUNT I—Conspiracy to Receive Embezzled Government Property (18 U.S.C. PP 371)

After the Pollards returned from their honeymoon in late summer of 1985, Mrs. Pollard began working for CommCore. The principals of that company were interested in breaking into the Washington market, with special emphasis placed on foreign government embassies. The firm specialized in media, lobbying and corporate training, and it was Mrs. Pollard's responsibility to attract new clients in the Washington area who could avail themselves of such expertise.

The People's Republic of China (PRC) had recently announced that it was seeking to become more Westernized and modernized. As part of that effort, the PRC wanted to improve its image among the American people and within the American business community. CommCore's CEO, Karen Berg, asked Mrs. Pollard to attempt to secure an appointment with one of the officials at the PRC's embassy in Washington, in order to demonstrate how CommCore could assist the PRC to improve its image. Mrs. Pollard informed Ms. Berg of her (Mrs. Pollard's) father-in-law's[5] acquaintance with the Chinese ambassador; and later, through Dr. Pollard, Mrs. Pollard received an official introduction to the Chinese ambassador. Consequently, she and her CommCore colleagues were invited to make a public relations presentation to certain members of the embassy staff in September of 1985.

In her effort to secure the embassy as a client, Mrs. Pollard determined to learn as much as possible about the PRC and its business, cultural and diplomatic relationships with the United States, including, of course, the embassy in Washington. To that end, she asked Mr. Pollard if he could bring home from work some articles containing general background information on China. Instead, Mr. Pollard brought home five separate documents, each marked "secret," which described the organizational structure of the various PRC consulates and embassy and gave biographical information about key Chinese diplomats. The five documents were: (1) People's Republic of China, Embassy—Washington, D.C. 1984 (73 pages); (2) People's Republic of China, Mission to the United Nations—New York, 1984 (35 pages); (3) People's Republic of China, Consulate—San Francisco, 1984 (47 pages); (4) People's Republic of China, Consulate—New York City, 1984 (46 pages); and (5) People's Republic of China, Consulate—Houston, 1984 (62 pages) (collectively "the PRC documents").6

The PRC documents admittedly contained certain classified information which would not normally be available to the public. However, as Mrs. Pollard skimmed through them and took notes for use in structuring her presentation, she ignored the classified portions of the PRC documents, because they dealt with matters in which she was not interested. She did not make any notes on the classified portions of the PRC documents. After finishing with them, Mrs. Pollard gave the PRC documents back to Mr. Pollard to return to his office.

On the day of the scheduled meeting at the embassy, September 30, 1985, Mrs. Pollard met with her two colleagues from Comm-Core, Ms. Berg and Andrew Gilman, who planned to accompany her at the presentation. She briefed them about the PRC, its potential public relations needs, and the various offices within the embassy with which they might work, without revealing that she had learned some of the background information from classified documents. The three CommCore representatives then met with several members of the embassy staff to discuss a public relations program. Ultimately, despite their efforts, CommCore did not obtain the PRC embassy as a client.

A subsequent government investigation confirmed that Mrs. Pollard did not disclose any classified documents or information to her colleagues or to any representative of the People's Republic of

China. The investigation included, among other things, interviews with the CommCore principals and a polygraph examination of Mrs. Pollard.

B. COUNT II—Accessory After the Fact to Possession of National Defense Documents (18 U.S.C. PP 793 (e) and 3).

On Monday, November 18, 1985, the Pollards planned to dine with Colonel Sella and his wife, Judy, who were visiting Washington. Mr. Pollard called his wife at 5:00 P.M. to tell her he was on his way home, but two hours later he had still not arrived. Mrs. Pollard became concerned, imagining a car accident or some other calamity causing her husband's delay. She called her husband's office several times, but was repeatedly told that he had left at 5:00 P.M. Shortly thereafter, Mrs. Pollard received a call from Mr. Pollard, saying he had to work late, which she knew to be untrue. In fact, unbeknownst to Mrs. Pollard, Mr. Pollard was with FBI and NIS agents, who were interviewing him concerning his unauthorized removal of classified materials from his office. In the telephone conversation with his wife, conducted within earshot of the federal agents, Mr. Pollard explained that he would be late for dinner and told her to take the "cactus"[7] to their friends at dinner. Mr. Pollard called again a few moments later, still in the presence of his interviewers, and again reminded Mrs. Pollard to take the "cactus" to their friends.

Recognizing that her husband was in some kind of trouble, Mrs. Pollard reacted to her husband's plea for help and quickly gathered up from the apartment the classified documents of which she was aware,[8] including the PRC documents. She placed them in a suitcase (not the briefcase in which Mr. Pollard regularly transmitted them) and proceeded down to the back door of her apartment building. As she started out the door, however, she saw several cars stopped in the alley with the motors running. She was not sure of the identity of the people in the cars, but, frightened, she retreated into the building and placed the suitcase underneath the basement landing of the stairs.

At a loss as to how to get the suitcase out of the building and fearful of leaving the documents unattended under the stairs, Mrs. Pollard went to the apartment of the Pollard's best friends and next-door neighbors, Babak and Christine Esfandiari. Indicating that the suitcase was too heavy for her to carry, Mrs. Pollard asked them to retrieve the suitcase from the stairwell and to bring it to her at the Four Seasons Hotel. When she failed initially to impress upon her friends the need to act immediately, Mrs. Pollard told them that she had a feeling that something had happened to "Jay" (Mr. Pollard) and, finally, that the suitcase contained classified documents that Mr. Pollard had brought home from work for her to use in preparation for her PRC embassy presentation. Mrs. Pollard then went to the Four Seasons Hotel and waited but did not see either of the Esfandiaris. Upon telephoning them on several occasions, she learned that Mr. Esfandiari had gone to the hotel but had been unable to find Mrs. Pollard. The suitcase was back in the Esfandiaris' apartment.

Still at the Four Seasons Hotel, Mrs. Pollard telephoned Colonel Sella. She met him later that evening at O'Donnell's restaurant in Bethesda, Maryland, near the Holiday Inn where the Sellas were staying. At the restaurant, Mrs. Pollard told Colonel Sella that her husband was in serious trouble and that he had asked her to remove something from the apartment. Colonel Sella gave Mr. Yagur's telephone number to Mrs. Pollard, instructing her to call Mr. Yagur if her husband was in fact in trouble. When she returned to the apartment after midnight, Mr. Pollard was there with several FBI and NIS agents, who were conducting a search of the apartment and seizure of certain classified documents.

Late the following day, Tuesday, November 19, 1985, the Esfandiaris contacted NIS about the suitcase. NIS contacted the FBI, which in turn went to the Esfandiaris' apartment to retrieve the suitcase. After obtaining a search warrant on Thursday, November 21, 1985, the FBI opened the suitcase and discovered the PRC documents and certain other classified documents.

IV. SUBSEQUENT EVENTS LEADING TO MRS. POLLARD'S ARREST

Subsequent to the events of the evening of November 18, 1985, Mr. Pollard submitted to additional interviews with FBI and NIS agents but was not arrested. Ultimately, he telephoned Mr. Yagur to explain that the Israelis would have to help him leave the country. Mrs. Pollard was thus faced with the prospect of fleeing the

United States with her husband or remaining behind to live the
remainder of her life without him. For her, the decision was virtually pre-determined. She loved the United States and considered
herself a patriotic American and felt she had no reason to flee the
country, but the thought of losing her husband was unbearable to
her. She and Mr. Pollard simply assumed she would leave with
him.

On the morning of Thursday, November 21, Mrs. Pollard underwent an outpatient medical procedure at Washington Hospital
Center for treatment of a rare stomach disorder.[9] Mr. Pollard accompanied her to the hospital. Afterwards, acting upon instructions from the Israelis, Mr. Pollard drove to the Israeli embassy and
entered through the open gates. It soon became obvious to the
embassy security force, however, that the FBI had succeeded in
following the Pollard car and was posted outside the embassy gates
watching their activity. Consequently, the embassy refused to admit the couple and demanded they leave the compound.

Once outside the embassy gates, Mr. Pollard was immediately
arrested by FBI agents. The agents also impounded Mrs. Pollard's
1980 Ford Mustang and seized two small bags in Mrs. Pollard's
possession. Although they did not arrest Mrs. Pollard, the FBI
agents effectively took her into their custody that afternoon. Three
FBI agents drove Mrs. Pollard to her apartment in an FBI car and
stayed with her for the next three to four hours. Several other
agents joined the group in the Pollards' apartment at various times.
After several hours, all of the FBI agents left Mrs. Pollard in the
apartment but not before taking her purse with them.

By the afternoon of the next day, Friday, November 22, 1985, FBI
and NIS agents had had the opportunity to interview Mr. Pollard
further and to search the suitcase taken from the Esfandiaris, the
bags seized from Mrs. Pollard outside the embassy, and the purse
seized from her later the same day.[10] Upon an analysis of the
classified documents in the suitcase, federal agents mistakenly
surmised that Mrs. Pollard's knowledge of the classified documents
was as intimate as her husband's. The FBI agents sought and
obtained a warrant for Mrs. Pollard's arrest later that afternoon.

At the same time, Mrs. Pollard was at the D.C. Jail with Mr.
Pollard's father, who had flown to Washington from Indiana upon
learning of his son's arrest. After some difficulty gaining admit-

tance to the jail, because virtually all of Mrs. Pollard's identification had been seized the previous day, the two did visit with Mr. Pollard. Afterward, as she and her father-in-law were leaving to go to dinner, Mrs. Pollard was taken into custody and formally charged with a violation of 18 U.S.C. PP 793 (e).

V. HEALTH

Since 1981, Mrs. Pollard has suffered from several different disorders of her gastro-intestinal tract, which worsened to severe conditions beginning in 1983. During that time, she has required frequent and regular medical treatment. In spite of that treatment, she has endured and continues to endure intense abdominal and chest pain, cramping, burning sensations, fever and nausea. As a result, she is unable to eat or digest her food properly for prolonged periods of time. Mrs. Pollard's doctors are only now beginning to understand some of her problems. Because she suffers from, among other things, a rather unique disease, the proper treatment and her recovery are uncertain.

One thing is certain, however. According to the treating physicians, Mrs. Pollard's rare condition will require frequent and regular monitoring. Considerable attention will have to be given to her diet and medications, and there is the potential that further surgery will be required. In the absence of such medical care, Mrs. Pollard's health will deteriorate further. We submit that she cannot and will not receive the proper medical care in prison and, as her doctors have indicated, that further incarceration would be detrimental to her health.

Mrs. Pollard began experiencing severe abdominal and chest pain, nausea and fever in 1983. As a result, she was hospitalized in October 1983 in Allentown, Pennsylvania where she was visiting her mother. At the time, the treating physicians suspected gall bladder disease, appendicitis, or infectious mononucleosis, but they were unable to determine the problem definitively. She was given antacids and antispasmodics and released without any successful relief from the pain.

The following February, in 1984, Mrs. Pollard was hospitalized at George Washington University Hospital for two weeks after suffering from similar symptoms. Despite numerous tests, the physicians were unable to diagnose the source of her pain. Subsequent consultations with numerous Washington-area physicians did not result in successful diagnosis or treatment of Mrs. Pollard's condition.

In June of 1984, Mrs. Pollard first began consultations with Dr. Herbert Moskovitz, an internist and gastroenterologist in Washington.[11] Dr. Moskovitz performed a battery of diagnostic tests which did not initially indicate Mrs. Pollard's condition. Subsequently, he performed an endoscopy[12] upon Mrs. Pollard which revealed, among other things, that her food, rather than passing out of her stomach through the digestive process, had formed into a large, indigestible mass known as a bezoar. Mrs. Pollard has suffered from the recurrent formation of bezoars since that time. Each time, the bezoar must be broken up by use of the endoscope. Additional endoscopies are also required to determine that the bezoar has completely dissipated.

In treating Mrs. Pollard, Dr. Moskovitz has determined that her problems are caused, in part, by abnormally delayed emptying of her stomach. This condition is treated primarily with medications that stimulate the stomach to empty or by surgery. If Mrs. Pollard does not receive these drugs in a regulated and timely fashion, her stomach fills up, resulting in vomiting and the release of acid from the stomach into the esophagus, causing inflammation. Because of the pain and swelling associated with the ulceration and inflammation of her esophagus and stomach, she cannot eat.[13]

Despite the diagnosis and subsequent treatment of Mrs. Pollard's stomach condition, she has continued to suffer severe pain and other uncomfortable symptoms, indicating the presence of some other untreated problem or problems. Mrs. Pollard's physicians performed tests to rule out the possibility of a pulmonary disorder; yet, her chest pains persisted. Dr. Moskovitz and others continued to suspect gall bladder disease, but traditional tests did not indicate any specific gall bladder disorder.

In July of 1986, Mrs. Pollard sought and obtained from the Court a modification of her conditions of release, allowing her to leave the Washington, D.C. metropolitan area for a medical consultation in Chicago. Through Dr. Moskovitz, an appointment was made for Mrs. Pollard in Chicago with Dr. Michael Goldberg, a specialist in biliary tract motility problems. Dr. Goldberg diagnosed Mrs. Pollard as having biliary dyskinesia, a condition of abnormal motility and pressures in the common bile duct. After treatment with medications was unsuccessful, Mrs. Pollard underwent multiple, complex surgical procedures at the University of Illinois in October of 1986. In addition to removing Mrs. Pollard's gall bladder, the surgeon, Dr. Robert Baker, enlarged the openings of her common bile duct and pancreatic duct into the intestinal tract. These procedures were designed to reduce pressure and relieve some of Mrs. Pollard's pain.

It does not appear that the surgery performed on Mrs. Pollard has been completely successful. She remains in a substantial amount of pain, and the doctors have speculated that the surgically enlarged openings have closed or will partially close due to scar tissue. In any event, Mrs. Pollard continues to suffer from the symptoms of biliary dyskinesia. This disorder is very rare; in fact, Dr. Baker, one of the few surgeons in the country to operate on biliary dyskinesia patients, had operated on only 20 such patients before Mrs. Pollard. Treatment is still somewhat experimental. Further surgery may be required.

At the present, Mrs. Pollard, despite treatment with several medications, experiences severe pain, bouts of nausea and vomiting, burning inflammations of her digestive tract, and resulting general weakness. This discomfort, combined with (and no doubt aggravated by) the stress of the events of the last year, has taken its toll on Mrs. Pollard's health. Since November 1985, she has lost nearly 60 pounds. If incarcerated, she would, in her physicians' opinions, be a difficult medical problem for the institution at best, and her condition could deteriorate significantly.

VI. INCARCERATION

Following her arrest, Mrs. Pollard was brought before a magistrate for a hearing on probable cause and pretrial detention. As a result of the pretrial detention hearings and the appeal therefrom, Mrs. Pollard was detained on the mistaken premise that she had knowledge of classified information and contacts with foreign governments—specifically, the PRC—for receipt of that information. The Court found that, if released, she would be likely either to flee the jurisdiction by seeking the sanctuary of a foreign country or to endanger the United States by further transferring classified information. Nothing could have been further from the truth. Nonetheless, Mrs. Pollard was remanded to the custody of the District of

Columbia Jail for 95 days, until February 24, 1986. Her incarceration was marked by severe physical and emotional suffering.

Mrs. Pollard's medical problems, for which she had undergone a surgical procedure the day before her arrest, were far from over. Rather, her condition worsened dramatically in jail. Initially, she was deprived of the medication on which she depended to regulate her condition. The reluctance of certain jail personnel to provide her with the proper medication was inexplicable. Even after she began to receive some of her prescriptions, she often failed to receive them at the proper times and frequencies. The jail food, lack of activity, and the extreme stress of being arrested and of being separated from her husband further aggravated Mrs. Pollard's condition. She endured long periods of constant pain and was frequently unable to eat. Her frequent requests for medical treatment went largely ignored, particularly because the jail's medical staff was unable to determine the cause of her condition. Finally, shortly before her release, Mrs. Pollard was admitted to the prison wing of the adjoining D.C. General Hospital, where a number of diagnostic tests, including a colonoscopy, were performed. Nevertheless, her severe discomfort continued. In the three months of her incarceration, Mrs. Pollard lost 40 pounds, while her hair began to turn gray.

Mrs. Pollard suffered emotionally as well. The humiliation at being branded as a heinous spy was great. In initial court appearances, the government had attached sinister motives to Mrs. Pollard's meeting at the PRC embassy, suggesting that she was passing intelligence information to the Chinese. In addition, the prosecutors initially argued that Mrs. Pollard was knowledgeable about the classified information Mr. Pollard was transferring and may herself have participated in his activities. These allegations, embellished in press accounts, portrayed Mrs. Pollard as a traitorous, unloyal American who had sold out her country. Friends and even family members expressed shock, outrage, disgust and hatred. Most abruptly disassociated themselves from Mrs. Pollard, not waiting for the vindicating news that she had not passed classified information to any foreign government and that she had had limited knowledge of Mr. Pollard's activities.

Mrs. Pollard continued to read press accounts that casually referred to her as a "spy," which hurt her deeply. The taunts and threats of her fellow inmates, who themselves looked down on the "spy" and the "Jew bitch," reinforced her ignominy. She realized she would never recover fully from the damage to her reputation, either personally or in her public relations career.

Mrs. Pollard felt the separation from her husband keenly. Initially, Mr. Pollard was held in the D.C. Jail as well, although he was soon transferred to the federal facility at Petersburg, Virginia. Even when her husband was in the same facility, however, Mrs. Pollard was not permitted to see him or to speak with him, even by telephone. Although it was possible for the Jail Chaplain to arrange such visits, as he had for other inmates with loved ones who were also incarcerated, there was a reluctance to do so for the Pollards, apparently because they had been charged with espionage. For over three months, when Mrs. Pollard was incarcerated, she saw her husband only once. The long period of separation and the uncertainty over her own and her husband's fate enhanced Mrs. Pollard's anxiety over the realization that they might be apart for many years to come.

Mrs. Pollard had virtually no other human contact to divert her attention from her physical pain and mental stress. At her own request, she had been placed in protective custody, separated from the other inmates, the vast majority of whom were being held on drug or prostitution charges. Because she was the only female inmate in protective custody, however, there were insufficient personnel and facilities to enable Mrs. Pollard to move about outside of her cell, to exercise, to watch TV, to make telephone calls, to read or to do laundry as the other inmates could. Instead, she was effectively placed in solitary confinement in her dirty, windowless cell, allowed out only for an occasional half-hour period a day when the other inmates were in their cells. Further, any conversation with the other inmates, even through the bars of her cell, was strictly forbidden by most of the guards.

Meanwhile, in the three months following Mrs. Pollard's arrest, the government gleaned substantially more information about the Pollards' cases. From its investigation, including a polygraph test administered to Mrs. Pollard, the government learned that Mrs. Pollard had not passed any classified documents or information to the Israelis or to the Chinese and did not have either the capacity or the inclination to do so. Therefore, the government admitted that Mrs. Pollard did not present a serious threat of fleeing the jurisdiction or endangering society, and pretrial detention was no longer justified.

VII. CONDUCT FOLLOWING RELEASE

Mrs. Pollard was released from custody on February 24, 1986, conditioned upon the posting of an unsecured bond for $23,500. In addition, she pledged to refrain from committing any local, state or federal offense; to refrain from leaving the Washington, D.C. metropolitan area, except to visit her husband wherever he might be incarcerated; to telephone the D.C. Pretrial Services Agency daily; to visit the D.C. Pretrial Services Agency in person weekly; to reside within the D.C. metropolitan area; and to seek employment actively. Finally, Mrs. Pollard agreed to a limited waiver of her Speedy Trial rights and granted the government an extension of time in which to return an indictment. As part of that waiver, both Mrs. Pollard and the government agreed to cooperate in the exchange of information through reciprocal discovery, in contemplation that this case could be resolved through a plea agreement.

Following her release, Mrs. Pollard did report, both by telephone and in person, as required and abided by the other restrictions on her release from custody. She also sought and obtained employment virtually immediately following her release from custody. Initially, unable to obtain permanent full-time employment, Mrs. Pollard performed temporary secretarial work through a temporary services agency in Washington, D.C. In March, she began permanent employment as an editorial associate for a service company located in downtown D.C. and began performing consultant work for the chief executive officer of a large public relations firm with its national headquarters in New York City. Both of these positions entailed public relations work, thus continuing the public relations career upon which Mrs. Pollard had embarked before her arrest in November of 1985.

Throughout the period following Mrs. Pollard's release from custody, she cooperated fully with federal prosecutors and investigators in their on-going investigation of the espionage activities of her husband. In particular, she explained the little she knew of Mr. Pollard's activities and her own lack of involvement to a polygraph examiner, who certified the truthfulness of her responses.

On June 4, 1986, Mrs. Pollard and her husband both appeared before Chief Judge Aubrey Robinson to tender guilty pleas. The

Court accepted Mrs. Pollard's plea to a two-count information charging her (a) with conspiring to receive embezzled government property, in violation of 18 U.S.C. PP 371, and (b) as an accessory after the fact to unauthorized possession of national defense information, in violation of 18 U.S.C. PP 193(e) and 3. Each count carries a maximum sentence of five years.

Mrs. Pollard's plea was entered pursuant to an agreement reached with the United States Attorney's Office. As part of the plea agreement, the United States Attorney's Office agreed not to oppose the imposition of concurrent sentences on the two counts. In addition, under the agreement, Mrs. Pollard agreed to submit to further interviews and polygraph tests as requested by the government and to testify before any grand jury, trial or other proceeding in this matter, responding fully and truthfully in all cases. She agreed to turn over to the government any property (including her engagement ring), documents or information in her possession relevant to the investigation and in general to comply with all reasonable requests from the authorities with respect to any specific assistance which she could provide. Both Mrs. Pollard's and Mr. Pollard's plea agreements were contingent upon complete compliance by the other to his or her agreement.

After the entry of her guilty plea, Mrs. Pollard continued her cooperation with authorities, including, among other things, meeting with agents of the FBI and NIS. In two intensive meetings in June and July, Mrs. Pollard described in detail the two trips the couple took abroad, relating all she could recall of each social contact she had had with Colonel Sella, Mr. Yagur, "Uzi," and their wives. She explained the little that she knew of Mr. Pollard's espionage activities and described the events giving rise to the offenses to which she had pleaded guilty. Mrs. Pollard also appeared and testified truthfully before the grand jury on July 3, 1986. Given that the information provided by Mrs. Pollard corroborated the government's case and established the facts surrounding the events of November 18, 1985, the quality and extent of her cooperation cannot be devalued.

On July 23, 1986, this Court granted Mrs. Pollard's motion to modify her conditions of release. As a result, she was permitted to travel beyond the Washington area to receive necessary medical care unavailable in the District of Columbia and to visit family members.

In August, Mrs. Pollard left the job she had begun in March because the company for which she was working closed its doors, apparently due to financial problems. She continued to work full-time, however, interrupted by periods when she was incapacitated by her medical condition, including periods of hospitalization. Mrs. Pollard worked again for a temporary services agency, usually assigned to a given office for at least a week at a time. In addition, Mrs. Pollard performed freelance work for her father's public relations endeavors. In November, after she returned from undergoing major surgery in Chicago, Mrs. Pollard obtained employment with a computer software manufacturer and distributor in Vienna, Virginia, which position she held until mid-January. At that time, she resigned to devote full time and attention and to assist counsel in their preparation for sentencing in this case. She plans to resume work immediately; indeed, her financial condition mandates that she continue working, since she has no savings and faces extensive outstanding medical and legal bills. 14

VIII. THE GOVERNMENT'S SENTENCING MEMORANDUM

From the inception of this case, when the government mistakenly insisted that Mrs. Pollard conspired to provide the PRC with information relating to the national defense, to its conclusion, when the government erroneously argues that Mrs. Pollard is "a mercenary driven by need and greed, a willing partner in crime," the government has attempted to twist the facts with its own inflammatory rhetoric in an attempt to persuade the Court by innuendo and unsupportable inference. For some reason—perhaps because the facts do not warrant it—the government appears to be on a crusade to insure that Mrs. Pollard is incarcerated further. Consequently, lest the government's mischaracterizations be left unchallenged, it is necessary to address its charges and to clarify the record.

The government begins its account of Mrs. Pollard's conduct by stating that Mr. Pollard frequently discussed Israeli politics with her. Surely, it has been made clear by the free admissions of both of the Pollards that Mr. Pollard was not only an ardent Zionist, but also was extremely knowledgeable about the entire Middle East region, reading about it voraciously and discussing it frequently with his wife and friends. Rather than giving rise to the inference that Mrs. Pollard conspired with her husband to provide the Israelis with classified information, the fact of Mr. Pollard's frequent discussion of Israel only serves to underscore the degree to which Mrs. Pollard respected her husband's knowledge and understanding of Israel and could readily accept his judgments about the country. Nor can it be discounted that Mrs. Pollard is an American Jew who was sensitive to such judgments. The government does not say—and it cannot say—that Mr. Pollard told his wife he was planning to transfer classified documents to Israel. Instead, the government can only point to general political discussions and to Mr. Pollard's statements that he was going to meet with "someone" to discuss how he (Mr. Pollard) might be of some help to Israel and hope that negative inferences—e.g., that Mrs. Pollard was involved in Mr. Pollard's initial decision to provide the Israelis with classified information—will be drawn by the Court at sentencing. The Court should summarily reject such inferences.

Next, in order to imply that Mrs. Pollard was involved in the planning stages of Mr. Pollard's scheme, the government describes in detail a visit by the Pollards to a friend's apartment, which the government alleges occurred in the summer of 1984. The government alleges that, in the course of this visit, Mrs. Pollard and her husband jointly attempted to recruit the friend to participate in Mr. Pollard's activities. However, the government's account of this visit, based on the account of the "friend," is simply inaccurate and untrue. It represents the use of incredible information to make a serious allegation of criminal conduct without any safeguards of reliability. In contrast to the unchallenged account of the friend, Mrs. Pollard's explicit denial that she ever attempted to recruit anyone on behalf of her husband has been certified as a truthful statement by the government's polygraph examiner. Although this express refutation of the friend's account should suffice, we take some time here to point out the inherent inconsistencies in the friend's account, due to the seriousness of the allegations involved.

This friend's name first came to light in this case when, in the course of one of Mr. Pollard's numerous interviews with investigators, Mr. Pollard was asked to name everyone who had any knowledge of his operation. This friend was, in fact, aware of Mr. Pollard's activities, but not by virtue of this visit of the Pollards to his apartment. The true version of that visit is as follows:

The Pollards went to visit their friend on a Saturday evening in the spring of 1984, hoping to persuade him to go out to dinner with them. Mr. Pollard had not yet been contacted by Colonel Sella; he had only been told by his New York friend that the New York friend had recently met an Israeli who might be interested in contacting Mr. Pollard. Thus, as the government writes with some understatement, Mr. Pollard's efforts to aid Israel were "still unrefined."

It is true that Mr. Pollard attempted to solicit his friend's participation in whatever might come of Mr. Pollard's initiative to work for the Israeli government. Mr. Pollard had envisioned that he might, at some point, need someone to travel to New York when he (Mr. Pollard) would be unable to do so, and it was for this sort of task that he sought his friend's help. Consequently, in vague terms, Mr. Pollard and his friend discussed a proposal to aid the Israelis. However, the transfer of classified documents was not mentioned, since Mr. Pollard did not know at that time that that would be required. Mrs. Pollard did accompany her husband to the friend's apartment and apparently overheard parts of it.

There was no discussion of "payment" for the friend. Indeed, there could not have been. Mr. Pollard had not yet begun any relationship with the Israelis and so, of course, knew nothing about any potential monetary compensation. Furthermore, Mr. Pollard himself did not receive any monetary compensation until the following November, when he finally accepted payments at the Israelis' insistence. Rather, the friend broached the subject of whether he would be paid for travel expenses, at which point Mr. Pollard said he assumed that the friend would be reimbursed.[15]

The remainder of the friend's account of the conversation makes even less sense than the premature "payment" issue. Disjointed quotes about "Anne's going into business for herself" and Mr. Pollard's proposed plan being "for the Brothers" (meaning the Israelis) are strung together as if there were a relationship there. What that relationship could possibly be is a mystery that even the government does not attempt to explain. Subsequent facts demonstrate that Mrs. Pollard did indeed launch an independent public relations career in mid-1985. She was contemplating such a move to freelance work as early as the previous summer of 1984, and she or Mr. Pollard may have mentioned the idea in casual conversation with the friend on this visit or on other occasions. However, there is no evidence that discussions of her "going into business for herself" could refer to anything else, particularly as relates to her husband's then "still unrefined" desire to do some kind of work for the Israelis. Nothing in the investigation of this case suggests that Mr. Pollard ever intended his wife to participate in his espionage activities, and the government has conceded, in its plea agreement, that Mrs. Pollard "did not personally deliver or disclose any national defense information to a foreign national." Moreover, it is illogical to suggest that the Pollards were about to embark on a sinister scheme together and in the next breath to suggest that Mrs. Pollard's going into business for herself was equally sinister.

Mrs. Pollard's lack of involvement in the whole scheme is notable, demonstrated by the fact that the next day, the friend demanded to meet with Mr. Pollard alone, without Mrs. Pollard's knowledge, to learn more details and, ultimately, to decline to participate. If the friend had actually been given the impression on the previous day's visit that Mr. Pollard and Mrs. Pollard were "in it together," it would have been illogical for him to insist on the exclusion of Mrs. Pollard at this subsequent meeting.

The friend's account of his statement to Mr. Pollard that, if Mr. Pollard was really serious, then he (the friend) felt he had no choice but to go to the federal authorities is not only self-serving but also disingenuous in the light of subsequent events. Although it is not made clear in the government's memorandum, Mr. Pollard discussed his espionage activities with the friend on a subsequent occasion, when the friend obtained knowledge about the actual nature and scope of what Mr. Pollard hoped to accomplish. In July of 1984, after Mr. Pollard had met with Colonel Sella, Mr. Pollard met his friend in Alexandria, Virginia and told the friend that he (Mr. Pollard) was meeting with a young military officer named Avi and was establishing channels for the transfer of classified information to the Israelis. These revelations were in response to the friend's specific inquiry about how Mr. Pollard's effort was progressing. The friend then kept this secret for 16 months and did not come forward to federal authorities even after Mr. Pollard's arrest.

The credibility of the friend is undermined not only by the inherent contradictions and illogical inferences in his account of the Pollards' visit, but also by his need to ingratiate himself with the government. At best, he is piecing together bits and pieces of various conversations he had with the Pollards together [sic] and with Mr. Pollard alone to reconstruct events, but he is utterly failing to do so accurately. At worst, his account now is an effort to relieve himself of any culpability for his own inaction.

Furthermore, the friend's story is contradicted by the Pollards' account of the visit, and by their insistence, verified by separate polygraph examinations, that Mrs. Pollard never attempted to "recruit" anyone. The friend has not submitted to a polygraph examination; he has not been cross-examined. The Court should discount the friend's version of events, as used by the government, as inherently untrustworthy and incredible.

The government again relies on innuendo and inference to draw a sinister picture of Mrs. Pollard's social contacts with the Israelis with whom her husband was dealing, both on two trips abroad, in the fall of 1984 and the summer of 1984 [sic], respectively, and in Washington, D.C. It is true that, although she was kept in the dark as to the substance of her husband's clandestine meetings, Mrs. Pollard was aware that the purpose of the trips abroad was for her husband to meet with certain Israelis outside the United States. When Mr. Pollard told her that she should go with him and that the trip would be at the Israelis' expense, she agreed. As a result, Mrs. Pollard undeniably benefited from her husband's activities, in that she had two nice vacations with him. However, there is no other significance to the trips vis-a-vis Mrs. Pollard, despite the great detail in which they are described by the government.

It is true that the wives of Mr. Pollard's contacts "babysat" Mrs. Pollard in Paris in 1984 and in Tel Aviv in 1985. It is also true that the Pollards went out to dinner as a couple with the Israelis and their wives on those and other occasions. However, the government does not allege, nor can it, that any of the Israelis ever revealed any information about the operation to Mrs. Pollard or that the Israelis even suspected that Mrs. Pollard knew the limited amount that Mr. Pollard had told her.

The government's memorandum implies that Mrs. Pollard's ignorance was a game that both sides played out, "the masks dropping only at the very end." It is not clear to what the government is referring in this statement. Even when Mrs. Pollard went to Colonel Sella on November 18, 1985, after the Pollards had failed to meet the Sellas for dinner as planned, she did not indicate any knowledge of her husband's activities nor did Colonel Sella assume any on her part. In fact, as the government's own account makes clear, Mrs. Pollard had great difficulty even convincing Colonel Sella that something was wrong. He responded only by giving her a telephone number.

Furthermore, it was sheer coincidence that Mrs. Pollard was even able to contact Colonel Sella on November 18, 1985. The previous evening, Mr. Pollard had told her that if he ever referred to the "cactus," it would mean that he was in trouble and that she should get the classified documents out of their apartment and contact Colonel Sella, Mr. Yagur, or the friend in New York City who had originally introduced Mr. Pollard to Colonel Sella. Significantly, however, Mrs. Pollard in fact had no means of contacting Sella or Yagur. Consistent with her lack of involvement in her husband's activities, Mrs. Pollard did not have phone numbers or addresses for these men. She only would have been able to contact the New York friend, who was a long-time personal friend of Mr. Pollard's family. It was only because Colonel and Mrs. Sella were visiting Washington and staying in a hotel in Bethesda that Mrs. Pollard was able to contact Colonel Sella.

While the government's account of the facts surrounding Mrs. Pollard's public relations presentation at the PRC embassy is, for the most part, technically accurate, the government seeks to bootstrap its case against Mrs. Pollard onto the case against Mr. Pollard by implying that she was in cahoots with Mr. Pollard in some sinister plot involving the PRC. As the facts do not support such an inference, the government's attempt at guilt by association should be vigorously rejected.

Mrs. Pollard has pleaded guilty to conspiracy to receive embezzled government property because, when presented with the documents by her husband, she did in fact reluctantly agree to look at them. Her acceptance and quick reading of the documents represented the full scope of the "conspiracy." Contrary to the government's allegations, the conspiracy did not include an agreement between Mr. Pollard and his wife that she develop a business relationship with the PRC. Rather, it was the principal of the public relations firm with which Mrs. Pollard was associated, Karen Berg, who was eager to establish contacts at foreign embassies in Washington. Ms. Berg was particularly interested in the PRC, in part because she had recently traveled in the Far East and in part because the PRC, seeking to change its image in the West, was a good business opportunity. When Mrs. Pollard informed Ms. Berg that Mrs. Pollard's father-in-law had some acquaintances at the embassy, Ms. Berg urged Mrs. Pollard to secure an appointment there. Mr. Pollard played no role in setting up this business arrangement.

As the government states, Mrs. Pollard did ask her husband for general information to help her in her business venture. However, it is important to look at what the government does not say. If there were any evidence to suggest that Mrs. Pollard requested classified documents or even to suggest that she expected to receive classified information, the government would surely have made such allegations. It does not because it cannot.

The undeniable facts, borne out by interviews with Mrs. Pollard's CommCore colleagues and a reconstruction of Mrs. Pollard's notes, are that Mrs. Pollard did not request classified information, did not pay any attention to the classified portions of the documents that she received, did not take notes on any classified information, did not transfer any classified information to anyone, and did not remember in any detail any of the classified information she may have seen in the course of reviewing the documents. She simply used the documents as a source of information that likely could have been obtained from a public library or other publicly available sources. Mrs. Pollard does not deny that she committed a criminal offense in connection with her use of the PRC documents, but the government cannot argue by inference, innuendo or otherwise that she was, by virtue of her use of the PRC documents, involved in espionage with her husband.

Furthermore, the government makes much of Mrs. Pollard's alleged "retention" of the PRC documents, again without any factual support. While it is true that she "retained" the documents long enough to review them, Mrs. Pollard gave the documents to her husband to return to his office as soon as she was finished. For this, she cannot be faulted. Her acts demonstrate that Mrs. Pollard, rather than lacking concern for the possible compromise of the documents, as the government alleges, realized that she could not appropriately dispose of them and that they should be returned by Mr. Pollard. He may have delayed in doing so, but his delay hardly translates to willful retention on the part of Mrs. Pollard. The government's argument concerning the "retention" of the PRC documents is simply another example of how the government has twisted the facts to mischaracterize Mrs. Pollard's actions.

The government's factual account, fraught with these unfair implications, is then followed by a discussion that cleverly uses exaggerated generalizations to describe Mrs. Pollard's actions inaccurately. For example, the government points to "her cooperation with her husband in secreting and attempting to dispose of the classified materials present in their apartment, in particular her conduct with the suitcase." The clear implication is that her "cooperation" in "secreting and attempting to dispose of the classified materials" went further than "her conduct with the suitcase" when, in fact, it did not.

The government also states that it has "strong evidence" of Mrs. Pollard's involvement in helping Mr. Pollard in his "use and secreting" of classified documents, yet the evidence it cites consists solely of Mrs. Pollard's removal of the suitcase and efforts to enlist the aid of her neighbors on November 18 and the fact that there were classified documents in the couple's apartment. The government insists that, because some of these documents "were in immediate proximity to Anne Henderson Pollard's belongings" within the apartment and because others bore her fingerprints (after she admittedly gathered some of them into the suitcase during the evening of November 18), they serve "to place her within the web of Jonathan Jay Pollard's criminality." We vigorously disagree. She never participated in obtaining, copying or delivering documents or information to the Israelis; and clearly, except for the PRC documents, she did not "use" them.

The evidence supporting the government's other allegations is no stronger. The government calls Mrs. Pollard a "mercenary," "motivated by need and greed." "Mercenary" implies that Mrs. Pollard was selling her services to someone. Yet, her only "service" was her eleventh-hour attempt to aid her husband in response to his call for help, an act not at all motivated by monetary compensation (nor one that would have been monetarily compensated), but rather one prompted by love.

Finally, the government has blown the issue of monetary compensation entirely out of proportion by its repeated, overused references to "luxury." A closer look at the impact of Mr. Pollard's compensation from the Israelis on the couple's lifestyle reveals no such luxury, nor even enough income to be a motivating force behind Mr. Pollard's actions. There is no doubt—and Mrs. Pollard does not deny, as the government suggests—that the Israelis financed two trips abroad for the Pollards and that they purchased a ring for Mr. Pollard to give to Mrs. Pollard as an engagement ring. In addition, they paid Mr. Pollard a total of $22,000 in monthly payments, $1,500 per month for eight months and $2,500 per month for the last four months up until his arrest.

Certainly this was enough to make life comfortable for the Pollards. Both relatively young and in the early stages of their careers, the two were earning combined salaries of approximately $50,000 a year. They shared a modest two-bedroom apartment and a 1980 Mustang car. On their income, living in downtown Washington, D.C., they had to monitor optional expenses carefully, especially after paying student loan fees and substantial uninsured medical expenses. Spending the additional income Mr. Pollard was receiving was easily accomplished without approaching "luxury." An analysis of the couple's financial records, including checkbook and credit card receipts, shows that the money went overwhelmingly to inexpensive lunches and dinners at the numerous casual, checkered-tablecloth eateries lining 19th and M Streets in downtown Washington or near the couple's home near Dupont Circle. Another sizable portion is indicated by relatively modest bills from Casual Corner, Syms, and similar moderately-priced clothing stores.[16] Undeniably, the Pollards enjoyed this extra money, but they hardly lived the life that is connoted by the government's emphasis on "luxury"—i.e., a life filled with swimming pools, mansions, fancy cars or furs.

Considering the unembellished facts, as described herein, it is inaccurate and unfair to generalize that Mrs. Pollard was a "willing partner in crime" who had an intimate familiarity with the substance of Mr. Pollard's espionage activities. And Mrs. Pollard has never suggested that she is "an innocent" or "a puppet manipulated and left to 'hold the bag.'" While such rhetoric makes good "copy" for the news media, to suggest it as a fact to the Court is inflammatory, at best. She has admitted her guilt and she has accepted responsibility for her actions, a fact which, along with her total cooperation with the government, the government unfairly tends to devalue.

IX RECOMMENDATION

Based on the totality of facts and circumstances relating to Mrs. Pollard and to the offenses to which she has entered guilty pleas, we recommend that the Court suspend the execution of any period of incarceration and place her on probation for a reasonable period of time.[17] In particular, Mrs. Pollard's youth and inexperience, her lack of any criminal record, the limited extent to which she participated in criminal conduct, her motivation in committing the offenses, and the victimless nature of her offenses all militate against incarceration. These same factors, as well as Mrs. Pollard's full cooperation with government authorities and her obvious ability and desire to resume her career and rebuild her life as a contributing member of society, suggest that probation is the most reasonable sentence. Finally and perhaps most importantly, Mrs. Pollard's ill health makes probation particularly appropriate, as probation will enable her to continue to receive the specialized medical care necessary to treat her condition.

It is important to note at the outset that this is not a case in which the court could sentence Mrs. Pollard to a term of years with confidence that she would in fact be released on parole before the termination of the full term of the sentence. The mechanics of the parole guidelines in this case would ensure that Mrs. Pollard would serve a substantial portion of any imposed jail term before being released. [19] Therefore, now is the time for the Court to acknowledge the substantial mitigating factors in Mrs. Pollard's case and to ensure that her sentence appropriately corresponds to the interests of punishment, deterrence, retribution and rehabilitation outlined below.

Mrs. Pollard's offenses consist of two acts which, while admittedly illegal, were not perpetrated with corrupt or malicious motivations nor part of a long-standing pattern of criminal activity on her part. One act involved her reading of reports supplied by Mr. Pollard from his office, which reports happened to contain irrelevant classified information, for her personal/business-related purposes. The second act involved her attempt to respond to a call for help from her husband. Both acts occurred because Mrs. Pollard, who had never committed any offense in the past, came to tolerate her husband's bringing home classified documents. We do not condone or justify her actions or pretend that what she did was right. Nevertheless, Mrs. Pollard's state of mind is highly relevant for sentencing purposes because it shows her general lack of moral turpitude and highlights the unlikelihood that Mrs. Pollard might commit a criminal offense in the future.

It is patently clear to anyone who has listened to Mrs. Pollard proudly describe her husband that she has an enormous amount of admiration for his intelligence and expertise in his field. In the course of their numerous discussions, Mrs. Pollard has responded to her husband's considerable insight not only with admiration but also with agreement with his ideals and with trust in his judgment. Mrs. Pollard's intellectual respect for Mr. Pollard has been heightened by her intense love for and emotional dependence on her husband. She has come to rely on Mr. Pollard's overwhelming concern for her and kindness to her. He is literally everything in the world to her. Thus, when Mr. Pollard justified his actions to his wife by emphasizing the service he was performing for Israel and assuring her that he was not harming the United States, she accepted his rationale.

In any event, there was little she could have done to stop him. Although she was extremely uncomfortable at the notion of her husband transferring classified documents, Mrs. Pollard continued to love and to believe in her husband. She had no desire or interest in participating in any way in Mr. Pollard's espionage, nor did Mr. Pollard want her to participate. However, it was only natural that, when Mr. Pollard cried out for help, Mrs. Pollard acted at his direction to remove the classified documents from their apartment.

Mrs. Pollard's actions reflect personal values which, in most [sic] any other context, would be considered socially and morally virtuous. The context in which Mrs. Pollard acted was not one of her own making, yet it rendered her largely automatic response criminal. While society has every right to prosecute and punish Mrs. Pollard for her offense, the punishment she has already suffered more than suffices to punish her for her limited involvement in Mr. Pollard's activities.

Mrs. Pollard's use of the PRC documents must similarly be viewed in the broader context of what was contained in those documents and how she came to receive them. Admittedly, the PRC documents are classified "secret," but the documents contain much general, publicly available information and only a limited amount of classified information. They are not documents, as the layman might speculate, that are full of detailed descriptions of missile defense systems or military placements. In fact, especially when compared to the documents in Mr. Pollard's case and when viewed in terms of how Mrs. Pollard used them, the PRC documents are relatively innocuous, a conclusion the Court may draw for itself from an in camera review of the documents.

Significantly, in anticipation of her presentation at the PRC embassy, Mrs. Pollard did not ask Mr. Pollard for classified documents. However, when she realized the documents could provide her with some of the background research she was seeking, she admittedly read through them. Because the documents contained little of the type of information that made them classifiable, Mrs. Pollard rationalized that she was doing "no harm." She did not focus on the classified parts of the reports; she did not take notes on those parts of the reports; and the government concedes that she did not relate any national security information to her public relations colleagues or to any PRC representatives.

Granted, the documents supplied by her husband saved Mrs. Pollard some time. Using the documents, rather than refusing to take advantage of them, was, at best, an exercise of bad judgment on Mrs. Pollard's part. To the extent she received the information and admittedly committed a criminal offense, Mrs. Pollard has already been sufficiently punished for that action.

Her punishment has taken several forms, all of which will have a lasting effect on Mrs. Pollard. First, Mrs. Pollard has been arrested and prosecuted and has pleaded guilty to two criminal offenses. Not only is she a convicted felon, but Mrs. Pollard has also become a household name since her arrest, branded in the newspapers and in the mind of the American public as a heinous "spy." Such labels will follow her the rest of her life. She, her family and her friends have suffered humiliation and public scorn. While she has diligently sought and obtained work since her release from custody, Mrs. Pollard must use her maiden name and refrain for the most part from drawing upon her past experiences for references, for fear that someone will reveal "who she really is." Because of her determination and perseverance, Mrs. Pollard will rebuild the bright career upon which she was embarked before her arrest, but it has suffered a set-back worth several years of progress. Socially, she is shunned by all.

Second, she has already spent three months in jail, marked by cruel and inhumane conditions, isolated in a cell for nearly 24 hours a day. Her needs for medication and proper health care went largely unmet, resulting in constant physical pain and a severe deterioration of her health. While in jail, Mrs. Pollard was unable to see her husband, the one person who means everything to her. Although she was a "model" prisoner in terms of her behavior, Mrs. Pollard did not tolerate jail well at all, suffering physically, emotionally and mentally. The thought of the possibility of returning has had a severe adverse effect on her health and her emotional stability.

Finally, Mrs. Pollard has suffered, and will long continue to suffer, from the separation of her husband. Because it is likely that Mr. Pollard will receive a jail sentence in this case, that separation will continue indefinitely. At the time of their arrests, the Pollards had been married for only three and a half months. They had hopes for raising a family and generally enjoying a long happy life together. Those hopes are gone. Granted, every wife suffers from the imprisonment of a husband. However, that fact does not negate the anguish felt by Mrs. Pollard, who can empathize with her husband's imprisonment because of the time she spent in jail. Nor does it render irrelevant the very real suffering that will be inflicted upon Mrs. Pollard in addition to her own punishment.

The government argues that a "strong signal" providing a "deterrent effect" is necessary. That signal has been sent and can be confirmed without the incarceration sought by the government. The harsh punishment which Mrs. Pollard has already endured and, indeed, continues to endure, more than suffices as a deterrence to anyone else who might feel tempted either to help a spouse engaged in illegal activity or to take advantage of the resources available to a government employee. Mrs. Pollard's case has clearly demonstrated that such a spouse is likely to be arrested and jailed and likely to be regarded in the same light, at least by peers and the press, with the more seriously offending partner. Surely, if Mrs. Pollard had been aware of the consequences that have already befallen her and her husband, she would not have acted as she did. The lesson of her experience has already been demonstrated, without any need for the additional punishment that would be imposed upon her by further incarceration.

No theory of retribution would support incarceration in this case either. The offenses committed by Mrs. Pollard are victimless. Her use of the PRC documents "hurt" no one. Because she received photocopies of the documents, the government was never deprived of possession of the originals or the information contained therein. It is clear that Mrs. Pollard neither used nor relayed any of the information contained in the documents that possessed the "secret" classification. Her attempt to help her husband was just that—an attempt. Therefore, there is no evidence of a security breach or damage to the United States resulting from Mrs. Pollard's acts.

The attempt of the government, in its "victim impact statement" included in the presentence report, to create victims where there are none, should be dismissed as mere puffery. It is yet another example of the government's overreaching attempt to make Mrs. Pollard's case something that it is not. Such dramatic exaggeration exposes the weakness of the government's allocution and its desperate desire to see Mrs. Pollard behind bars.

It is particularly disingenuous to characterize the "friend," who had deliberately inquired and learned about Mr. Pollard's activities yet kept silent for 16 months until named by Mr. Pollard, as a victim. Not only did the friend willingly keep himself informed of Mr. Pollard's activities, but he (the friend) had also previously participated in activities which the government, in its allocution memorandum in Mr. Pollard's case, uses to condemn Mr. Pollard.

Similarly, the neighbors, who only turned over the suitcase to the FBI when their attempt to deliver it to Mrs. Pollard failed, have not "suffered" as victims of any crime. They have not been threatened with prosecution, but rather have been portrayed as heroes in the government's papers. Their identity was scrupulously protected by the government, the defendants and defense counsel; yet, it was Ms. Esfandiari who chose to tell her story and be pictured in *The Washington Post* following the entry of the Pollard's pleas.

Finally, it is unfair to suggest that the "victims" of Mrs. Pollard's crimes are the same as her husband's crimes. Mrs. Pollard was not a co-conspirator to her husband's espionage or otherwise engaged jointly in that activity with him. The government is once again attempting to prosecute Mrs. Pollard via guilt by association, a ploy that this Court should soundly reject.

As a result of the punishment Mrs. Pollard has suffered—i.e., the three months of incarceration, the year of travel restrictions and reporting requirements, the ignominy of arrest and felony convictions, the damage to her reputation and career, her anxiety and fear of a possible return to jail, the separation from her husband, the deterioration of her physical and mental health, and the anxiety and anguish she feels for his imprisonment—she has had more than ample opportunity and incentive to reflect on her offenses and to suffer great remorse for committing any criminal act. Her experiences have demonstrated to her not only the full power that can be brought to bear in enforcing the laws of the United States, but also the importance of maintaining the sanctity of those laws, without placing one's moral intentions above them. Thus, she is already well along in the process of rehabilitation.

From the time of her arrest, Mrs. Pollard has demonstrated the utmost respect for and cooperation with prison officials, government investigators and prosecutors. She was a model prisoner at the D.C. jail, despite the severe medical difficulties she was enduring at the time, winning the respect of many of the guards and other prison authorities. Since her release from custody, Mrs. Pollard has complied with many conditions imposed on her release, remaining within the D.C. metropolitan area, maintaining employment and reporting to D.C. Pretrial Services by phone and in person as required.

Further, Mrs. Pollard has cooperated fully with the government investigation in this case. Even prior to reaching an agreement with the U.S. Attorney's office regarding a guilty plea in this case, Mrs. Pollard initiated such cooperation, submitting to polygraph examinations. Thereafter, she also participated in interviews with agents of the FBI and NIS and testified before the grand jury. In these sessions, she has detailed what she knew of her husband's operation, described his Israeli contacts and all the occasions on which she saw them when travelling abroad, and provided the details surrounding her use of the PRC documents. She has proven herself to be forthright throughout. As a result of her cooperation, the government received important corroboration of the facts supporting its investigation of Mr. Pollard and of both his American and Israeli contacts. This investigation is apparently continuing and may lead to further indictments. Most significantly, Mrs. Pollard has demonstrated her recognition of the wrongfulness of her actions, her willingness to cooperate with authorities, and her desire to spare the government the expense and necessity of a prolonged public trial by tendering a guilty plea to this Court. As a result, she has determined to place her faith, and her fate, in the American judicial system.

Placing Mrs. Pollard on probation, rather than sentencing her to a jail term, would be the best way for this Court to further Mrs. Pollard's rehabilitation. Indeed, incarceration would interrupt and hinder Mrs. Pollard's rehabilitation. As she has already demonstrated, both before her arrest and while released pending sentencing, Mrs. Pollard has a strong will to work and the capability both of supporting herself and of contributing to society. Her aptitude in public relations—her previous experience, her creativity, her writing ability, her skill in dealing with people—demonstrates strong promise for the successful resumption of her career, hampered only, of course, by her criminal record. A jail term would not only further delay Mrs. Pollard from resuming her career, but would also further damage her ability to obtain employment in her field.

Incarceration would also lead to a serious deterioration of Mrs. Pollard's physical, mental and emotional health. It is clear from the physicians who have treated her, including her gastroenterologist, Dr. Moskovitz, and the surgeon, Dr. Baker, who recently operated on her, that Mrs. Pollard suffers from gastro-intestinal problems that require frequent and immediate attention. It is even likely that further surgery will be required. We submit, in accordance with the reports of the treating physicians, that further incarceration would be detrimental to her health,[21] as it was when she was previously incarcerated after her arrest. In contrast, probation will give Mrs. Pollard the opportunity to receive (and to finance) the specialized care necessary to treat her medical condition.

Incarceration could also have a deleterious effect on Mrs. Pollard's emotional well-being, because it would likely prevent her from being able to visit or to telephone Mr. Pollard. Mrs. Pollard remains totally devoted to her husband and continues to draw much of her strength to deal with her situation from her ability to communicate with him, both personally and by telephone. While, as stated above, the separation imposed by Mr. Pollard's incarceration represents a great hardship for Mrs. Pollard, the total loss of any contact with Mr. Pollard that would result from [his incarceration] Mrs. Pollard might never recover [from].

Thus, whereas a period of incarceration would be a detriment to Mrs. Pollard's health, career potential, financial situation, emotional and mental state, and confidence in her ability to lead a productive life, probation would afford her the opportunity to live a productive, independent life. Mrs. Pollard has demonstrated great potential to reestablish herself as a successful, law-abiding person. She should be given that chance.

REFERENCES:

[1] Letters from Mrs. Pollard's supervisor at the Chemical Specialities Manufacturers Association and the National Rifle Association regarding Mrs. Pollard's employment performance are attached hereto.

2 One large expense which Mrs. Pollard and Mr. Pollard shared was the uninsured portion of her medical care costs, including prescription drugs. See Section V. Health, infra.

3 Mrs. Pollard later learned that, while in Paris, Colonel Sella arranged to purchase a diamond and sapphire ring that she had admired during one of the shopping trips with Colonel Sella's wife. Mrs. Pollard and Mr. Pollard had been shopping for an engagement ring for some time, and she was told by Mr. Pollard that the ring was intended as a wedding gift from the Israelis to the Pollards.

Subsequent to the guilty plea in this case, Mrs. Pollard, upon the government's request, turned the ring over to federal prosecutors.

4 While Mrs. Pollard admittedly knew that her husband was delivering documents to the Israelis, she never accompanied him on any of his "drops," nor did she ever participate in obtaining, copying or delivering any documents or information to the Israelis or to any representative of a foreign government.

5 Dr. Morris Pollard is a world renowned microbiologist who, through his work, had previously met the Chinese ambassador.

6 A detailed description of the contents of these five documents will be included in a supplemental memorandum which will be filed under seal with the Court.

7 Only the previous day, November 17, 1985, Mr. Pollard had told Mrs. Pollard that, if he were ever to use the word "cactus," it would mean that he was in trouble and that she should get the classified documents out of their apartment. Mr. Pollard had chosen the word arbitrarily as he was looking at the cactus plants in the couple's apartment.

8 Mrs. Pollard's lack of awareness of her husband's activities is demonstrated by the fact that she did not gather all of the classified documents that were actually in the apartment.

9 See Section V, HEALTH, infra. See also letters of Dr. Herbert Moskovitz, Dr. Michael Goldberg and Dr. Robert Baker submitted as attachments hereto.

10 No classified documents were found in Mrs. Pollard's bags or purse.

11 Dr. Moskovitz's letter to the Court, outlining his diagnosis and treatment of Mrs. Pollard, is attached hereto.

12 During an endoscopy, performed by the insertion of a long tube through the patient's mouth into the digestive tract, the physician can both see the internal organs through fiber optics and perform procedures such as biopsies or washing. Thus, endoscopy has both diagnostic and treatment functions.

13 While in D.C. Jail, prior to her release on bond, Mrs. Pollard did not receive the proper medication in a timely fashion or the proper type of food. As a result, she suffered greatly and lost approximately 40 pounds. Only through the efforts of Dr. Moskovitz and undersigned counsel was she ultimately able to receive some medical care at the D.C. General Lock Ward. However, the care she received was inadequate and did not relieve her problems.

14 For the past year, while free on bond, Mrs. Pollard has abided by restrictions that seriously curtailed her freedom, and she has responded to and satisfied each request

made by the government. At the same time, she has attempted, despite the demands of employment, medical care and her release restrictions, to remain in constant contact with her husband by daily conversations and weekly visits. All of this has taken its toll on her, both physically and mentally. All things considered, though, this past year has demonstrated not only that Mrs. Pollard has suffered as a result of her wrongdoing but also that she can and will abide by any reasonable conditions of probation which the Court may impose in this case.

15 The government's account of the visit implies that Mrs. Pollard and Mr. Pollard, motivated by monetary compensation, together tried to recruit the friend by promising him that he could "live better." This implication is in fact another example of totally innocent remarks taken completely out of context.

Upon their arrival at the friend's apartment, the Pollards did indeed criticize the friend for being stingy and anti-social. This was a standing joke between them. Mr. Pollard, in particular, frequently teased his friend about the friend's unwillingness to spend any money despite his comfortable accountant's salary. The barbs were intended that evening to provoke the friend to come out to dinner, rather than to eat the packaged macaroni and cheese dinner the friend had just prepared for himself.

16 Mrs. Pollard, while by no means maintaining an extravagant wardrobe, was frequently forced to purchase clothing in several different sizes because her medical condition resulted in dramatic variations in her weight.

17 Alternatively, the Court can impose a "split sentence," pursuant to 18 U.S.C. Pp 3651. If the Court finds a split sentence appropriate, we recommend that the Court suspend all but three months of a sentence of incarceration and provide for a probationary period thereafter. Under such a scheme, of course, Mrs. Pollard would receive credit for the three months she has already spent in jail. See 18 U.S.C. 3568.

As outlined above, the government does not oppose the imposition of concurrent sentences in this case. Concurrent sentencing is especially appropriate here, given the relationship between the two offenses, i.e., the use of the PRC documents and the subsequent attempt to dispose of the suitcase containing them.

18 Because probation will allow Mrs. Pollard to continue gainful employment, it will ensure that Mrs. Pollard will be able to afford and/or insure the medical care necessary for her condition.

19 For example, under Count II, the Parole Commission would base its decision on guidelines which assign the most severe "category eight" offense characteristic grade to all charges of "espionage and related offenses," despite the variance in maximum sentences allowed under 18 U.S.C. Pp 793 and 794. See Parole Comm'n Rules and Procedures Manual Pp 2.20. Paroling Policy Guidelines, Chapter 10, "Offenses Involving National Defense," p. 50. Under the guidelines, an accessory after the fact charge is graded two categories below the underlying charge, resulting in a "category six" offense classification on Count II of Mrs. Pollard's charges. Rules and Procedures Manual Pp 2.20, Chapter 1, Subpart 104, "Accessory After the Fact," p. 30. Consequently, although the maximum prison term for Count II is 5 years, the recommended time to be served by an offender with the best parole prognosis, such as Mrs. Pollard, would be 40–52 months on Count II alone. See Rules and Procedures Manual Pp 2.20, Guidelines Chart," p. 28

In the Presentence Report, U.S. Probation Officer Carlson, while noting that Mrs. Pollard's prognosis for probation is "excellent," estimates that the time to be served by Mrs. Pollard, if incarcerated, would be 100 months.

[20] Interestingly enough, in both its public sentencing memorandum and its in camera submission (damage assessment) to the Court in Mr. Pollard's case, the government does not assert that the American people were "victimized" by Mrs. Pollard. Indeed, no reference to Mrs. Pollard is made in the government's damage assessment.

[21] Considering all of the circumstances of this case, it would be shameful even to debate whether Mrs. Pollard could be placed in a prison hospital. There are too many reasons why she should not be imprisoned at all, irrespective of whether we believe there is a prison facility, hospital or otherwise, which could provide her with adequate medical care. To suggest otherwise would further expose the government's sole purpose in requesting incarceration—i.e., additional punishment.

LETTER TO ELIE WIESEL FROM JONATHAN JAY POLLARD

Petersburg, VA
January 27, 1987

Elie Wiesel
New York, NY

Dear Professor Wiesel,

After 14 months of internally debating the propriety of contacting you directly, I have decided to write in order to provide you with an explanation of why I felt compelled to undertake certain actions on behalf of Israel. Although subsequently refined in the crucible of a 9-foot by 6-foot cell, I feel that the thoughts set out below accurately reflect the preexisting values which formed the intellectual and emotional bases of my behavior and are not proffered either as an excuse or rationalization for the commission of a crime. However I should emphasize the distinction in my own mind between the violation of the laws of man and those of the God of Sinai and Joshua, against whom I do not believe I have transgressed.

In spite of the fact that I have been greatly troubled over how this whole affair has been mishandled by both the Israeli and American governments, I am nevertheless confident that what I did, however ill-advised it was in retrospect, will make a significant contribution to Israel's military capabilities. From my perspective, if this results in the saving of Jewish lives either during a war or by the prevention of one through the strengthening of Israel's deterrent capacity, then at least something good will have come from this tragedy.

You should understand that I was raised with the notion that each and every Diaspora Jew has an absolute obligation to act as one of the stones, so to speak, which comprise the modern day

outer battlements of Zion. Although this commitment usually man-
ifests itself through such conventional mechanisms as Aliya, financial support to and political lobbying on behalf of Israel, there may
be other highly unusual circumstances in which a Jew is forced to
apply situational ethics as a guide to his or her actions. In my case,
this complex and often agonizing intellectual process was somewhat simplified by the realization that the strengthening of Israel
would unquestionably improve America's strategic position
throughout the Middle East. In other words, Israel's gain would in
no way be America's loss—quite the contrary. I can also assure you
that this perspective was shared by all the Israeli officials with
whom I had the honor to work. Given the special relationship
between the two countries and the unparalleled opportunities this
country has provided our local Jewish community, how could any
responsible American Zionist even think of doing something
harmful to the United States?

Having said this, it is indeed unfortunate that due to all the
contrived sensationalism surrounding the case, both my motives
and instructions have been utterly distorted beyond recognition,
leaving the American public with the mistaken impression that
Israel had employed a mercenary to undertake activities designed
to damage the national security of the United States. Despite the
remote possibility that this grotesque misrepresentation of the operation may have been caused, in part, by the hysteria associated
with the spate of Soviet spies arrested this year, I can't help but
come to the disturbing conclusion that certain political elements,
opposed to the extraordinarily close relationship between Jerusalem and Washington, have been using this case as a means of
embarrassing the American Jewish community, Israel, and its allies
within the government. As I've repeatedly stated both on and off
the record, I am mortified that my actions have inadvertently
provided these local anti-Semites with an opportunity to wrap
themselves in the flag of respectability and to emerge from beneath
their rocks. I can only hope that with the eventual disclosure of the
truth, whatever perceived damage has been done to the standing of
the American Jewish community and Israel will be repaired. Just
please accept my word that the gains to Israel's long term security
were indeed worth the risks and that I would never have jeopardized either my life or my wife's health if I hadn't thought the
situation demanded it.

Perhaps you can understand my position in light of a Hebrew expression which has long been used to describe our only moral choice when it comes to issue of Jewish survival; *ein breirah*—no alternative. G-d, how I wish it had been otherwise, but it would have been an outright betrayal of my heritage, my personal integrity, and an entire family lost in the ovens of the Holocaust if I had simply taken the safe route and closed my eyes as to what had to be done. Years ago, Dr. Wiesel, I had closed my eyes for just a moment when I stood in the gas chambers of Dachau where my parents had come to say Kadesh over 75 members of our Lithuanian family, all of whom had simply been wiped off the earth as if they had never existed. It was at that precise moment that I swore before G-d that their slaughter would be avenged, not by my participation in the killing of anyone, but by the preservation of what remained of our people. Two years ago I was confronted by the "business end" of this obligation, which I could never have anticipated would result in yet a second, more personal Holocaust for our family.

I'm quite sure that you can appreciate the precarious nature of Israel's strategic situation in the Middle East and the fact that unexpected threats to the state's survival can materialize very rapidly with untold consequences—the existence of peace treaties, confidence building "understandings," and great power assurances of timely support notwithstanding. When it comes down to the wire and "the iron dice of war are rolled," as Ludendorff said, we stand alone and any one who believes to the contrary is either unaccountably ignorant of history or criminally naive. Thus when I realized that a whole new generation of ultra sophisticated military equipment was quietly being introduced into the arsenals of our most implacable enemies, without Israel being forewarned by her ostensively [sic] "loyal" allies. It was my fear that the conditions were being laid for a technological Pearl Harbor of such proportions that the Yom Kippur War would look pale in comparison. With Syria, in particular, able to commence hostilities at a moment's notice, I really didn't know whether I was observing a short fused time bomb or something more manageable. All I could say for certain, though, was that time, of whatever duration, ultimately translated out in terms of Israeli lives and acted accordingly.

When my wife, Anne, and I visited the Golan Heights in the summer of 1985, it was with a sense of guarded optimism that we looked across that forbidding escarpment at the distant Syrian positions and realized that we had at least attempted, however imperfectly, to guarantee the security of the exposed frontier settlements behind us. How the prosecution can turn around and assert that this behavior suggests the manifestation of an underlying amoral mentality on our part is extremely difficult for me to understand. But, then again, most of this case has been nothing short of a Kafkaesque nightmare for us.

Regrettably the issue of money has served to obscure my true motives in this affair which, until Mr. Blitzer's interviews in the *Jerusalem Post,* I had not been able to articulate publicly. While it is true that money did pay a role in certain operational aspects of my undertakings, this is not to say that I simply sold my soul to Mammon. As you are undoubtedly aware, affairs such as these necessarily require a great deal of logistical support, which is a fact of life not exactly self-evident to the average person on the street. Moreover given the rather jaded expectations of a society long grown accustomed to one dimensional "villains," it has been far easier for the prosecution to attribute simple pecuniary motives to a Jewish spy rather than complex ideological ones whose significance lies well beyond its pathetically limited powers of comprehension. In spite of having hard evidence explaining this particularly vexing aspect of the case, the Justice Department can't seem able to appreciate the fact that after much soul searching I attempted to repay my Israeli control without success—which is hardly the behavior of a cold blooded mercenary. For some reason beyond my comprehension, though, the prosecution is absolutely determined to overlook this aspect of my behavior and is intent on pounding away at my alleged moral bankruptcy for having taken financial compensation in the first place. But what was I supposed to do? I never expected this arrangement and when it took place I just assumed the professionals knew what they were doing. My trust has been twisted and perverted into something so horrendous that the ideals with which I started this operation have somehow been sacrificed on the altar of political expediency.

Closely related to this line of character assassination has been the equally charming piece of airtight disinformation concerning my "mental instability," which has been conveniently discovered by a prosecution trying desperately to discredit me. Efforts by my defense attorney to gain access to the records have been repeatedly denied and now we've been told that they may be missing. Well, perhaps with time and access to the facts, the attitude, or should I say malleability of the press will change with regard to my personal integrity. In the interim, though, I almost feel like one of the Refuseniks who, after being told that he must be "insane" for wanting to leave the socialist paradise, is promptly thrown into an asylum and forgotten about. When certain Justice officials told me that they would make it impossible for any American Jew to speak out in my defense, I never thought that they would be able to back this threat up by stealing a page from the KGB. Of course, I should have known better since these were the same officials who made sure my wife and I pleaded one day before a House vote was scheduled to decide whether or not to approve a Saudi arms package.

In many respects, however, Anne's ordeal has been far worse than mine since her severe physical problems were greatly complicated by the denial of proper medical attention while she was being held at the District of Columbia Jail—an institutional malignancy that could be unfavorably compared to such notorious prisons as Dartmoor and the Czarist fortress of St. Peter and St. Paul. You would never believe a detention facility like this actually exists in the United States unless you experienced it first hand: rats, snakes, swarms of insects, no heat, no light, no blankets or clean sheets, incessant noise, toilets that never work, daily pesticide foggings that leave one nauseated for hours, the constant presence of sewer gas, unpotable water, pathological guards, untreated AIDS carriers handling food trays, and an inmate population that reflects the most degenerate group of subhuman individuals ever collected under one roof. It is quite literally a level of hell that could have figured prominently in Dante's "Inferno." After three months of being totally locked down within this neurotic environment without ever being able to breathe fresh air, see the light of day or receive her medications until I started "cooperating," my wife was conditionally released due to her rapidly deteriorating health and the unjustified nature of her charges. During this period of time, Anne and I were not allowed to even see each other, which for a couple as close as we are was nothing short of torture. The daily news that I was permitted to hear about her was that the Hanafi Brotherhood had instructed their female counterparts to kill her if the opportunity presented itself. I suppose this is the type of "justice" to be expected from an administration which could turn a

Presidential visit to a Nazi cemetery into an attempt at placing a time limit on moral outrage.

Apart from our continued separation, which has been excruciating, life for Anne has been indescribably hard given her recurrent medical problems, the uncertainty of our future, and these horrendous allegations about our "life style," which have evidently been designed to destroy what little remains of our reputations. Needless to say, we are both extremely tired right now and are trying, as best we can, to prepare ourselves for a sentencing session which might result in our destruction as a couple. I can't even begin to adequately describe what kind of emotional pressures are produced by the painfully slow process of judicial crucifixion. In a sense, Anne and I feel as if we're aboard one of those sealed cattle cars pulling up to the separation platform from Auschwitz, while all about us the Jewish community just sits like mute spectators awaiting the fall of the axe. We scream and yell for help, but all we receive in return are the stolen glances of a people only capable of expressing the twin sentiments of empathy and impotency.

Assuming the court is merciful, we may yet live to reach Israel, but at the present time the prosecution is demanding our heads as an object lesson for others who might be similarly inclined to help Israel. We have been told to expect the worst because no one has summoned the community to put a stop to this ordeal. In the presence of such timidity, those officials at Justice who view this case as an opportunity to put Israel in her place by equating my actions with those of a Soviet spy will carry the day. Anne and I pray to G-d that somewhere a person will do for us what we tried to do for our people—barring that, we shall be forced to spend our days in a state of permanent exile like Moses atop Mt. Nebo. We have placed our fate in G-d's hands and hope this tragedy will not come to pass.

Sincerely,

Jonathan Pollard

ANNE HENDERSON POLLARD'S MEMORANDUM FOR REDUCTION OF SENTENCE

Anne Pollard respectfully submits this memorandum in support of her motion for reduction of sentence pursuant to Rule 35(b) of the Federal Rules of Criminal Procedure.

I. SUMMARY OF ARGUMENT

Reconsideration of the factors presented at sentencing, as illuminated by subsequent events, warrants a substantial reduction of Mrs. Pollard's sentence. Mrs. Pollard suffers, *inter alia,* from biliary dyskinesia—a painful and incapacitating physical disorder—which has not been, and cannot be, treated effectively during her incarceration. Consequently, continued incarceration delays for five years any opportunity for effective treatment of Mrs. Pollard's illness and dooms her to a severe and painful existence well beyond that contemplated by her sentencing. Indeed, the severity of Mrs. Pollard's sentence is so exacerbated by its impact on her health that she suffers more than others similarly sentenced.

Further, the circumstances underlying Mrs. Pollard's incarceration favor a reduction of her sentence. Mrs. Pollard admittedly committed two offenses for which she has suffered approximately seven months of incarceration, the ignominy of arrest and felony convictions, irreparable damage to her reputation and career, defamatory reports in the media, separation from her family, the steady deterioration of her physical health, and severe restrictions on her First Amendment rights. The actions which gave rise to her convictions were motivated neither by financial remuneration nor by an intent to harm the United States or to aid any foreign government. Rather, her criminal offenses were acts of poor judgment born out of love for and trust in her husband. Moreover, the offenses committed by Mrs. Pollard were victimless. Ironically, the victim, if any, is Mrs. Pollard who has been punished and will continue to be punished, whether in or out of prison, for her actions.

Moreover, reduction of Mrs. Pollard's sentence is appropriate in light of her valuable cooperation with the government and her good behavior since her arrest. Throughout this case, Mrs. Pollard has willingly shared her knowledge with government investigators, corroborated the information provided by her husband (to the extent she could), religiously abided by the stringent conditions of her release prior to sentencing, and complied with the conditions of her plea agreement. Similarly, Mrs. Pollard continues to be a cooperative, well-behaved prisoner despite her painful medical condition.

Finally, the government has attempted to influence the Parole Board with statements which misconstrue the facts in this case. Realistically considering the operation of the Parole Board, those statements have effectively ensured that Mrs. Pollard will not be released by the Parole Board before the expiration of her five year sentence. Consequently, now is the time for the Court to acknowledge the substantial mitigating factors in Mrs. Pollard's case and to exercise leniency in the reduction of her sentence.

II. HISTORY OF THE CASE

Mrs. Pollard was arrested on November 22, 1985, one day after the arrest of her husband, Jonathan J. Pollard, and charged with a violation of 18 U.S.C. § 793(e). Following a hearing on probable cause and pretrial detention, Mrs. Pollard was detained on the erroneous premise that she had knowledge of classified documents and contacts with foreign governments for the receipt of that information. Mrs. Pollard was placed in pretrial detention in the District of Columbia Jail for 95 days—a period marked by severe physical and emotional suffering resulting in part from a deprivation of essential medication and medical treatment.

Following her release from detention on February 24, 1986, Mrs. Pollard actively sought and obtained employment in the Washington, D.C. metropolitan area. In addition, during her release, Mrs. Pollard devoutly adhered to numerous reporting requirements and travel restrictions, which required, *inter alia*, daily telephone calls, and weekly visits, to the D.C. Pretrial Services Agency, and, with limited exceptions, prevented Mrs. Pollard from traveling outside the Washington, D.C. metropolitan area except to visit her husband wherever he might be incarcerated.

On June 4, 1986, Mrs. Pollard entered a plea of guilty to a two-count information, charging her with conspiracy to receive embezzled government property, in violation of 18 U.S.C. § 371, and as an accessory after the fact to her husband's possession of national defense information, in violation of 18 U.S.C. § 793(e) and 3. Mr. Pollard pleaded guilty to a single count indictment, charging him with conspiracy to deliver national defense information to a foreign government—to wit, Israel—in violation of 18 U.S.C. § 794(c). Mrs. Pollard's plea was entered pursuant to an agreement reached with the United States Attorney's Office. As part of that agreement, Mrs. Pollard agreed to submit to further interviews and polygraphs as requested by the government,[1] to testify before any grand jury, trial or other proceeding in this matter, to turn over to the government any property, documents or information in her possession relevant to the investigation, and to comply with all reasonable requests from the authorities with respect to any specific assistance which she could provide.

Mr. and Mrs. Pollard appeared before Chief Judge Aubrey Robinson for sentencing on March 4, 1987. Following statements by both the government and the defense, Chief Judge Robinson sentenced Mrs. Pollard to incarceration for a period of five years on each of the two counts, the terms to be served concurrently. The Court denied Mrs. Pollard's request for voluntary surrender. Instead, she was taken immediately to the Federal Correctional Institution at Lexington, Kentucky ("F.C.I. Lexington"), where she is currently serving her sentence. Mr. Pollard was sentenced to life imprisonment.

III. LEGAL STANDARDS GOVERNING THIS MOTION

Both the statute and case law governing reduction of sentence support Mrs. Pollard's motion. Rule 35(b) of the Federal Rules of Criminal Procedure provides in pertinent part:

Reduction of Sentence. A motion to reduce a sentence may be made . . . within 120 days after the sentence is imposed or probation is revoked. . . .

---

[1] Even before the entry of the guilty pleas, Mrs. Pollard cooperated with the government by submitting to various interviews and polygraph examination, *inter alia*, to confirm her lack of involvement in her husband's espionage activities.

The court shall determine the motion within a reasonable time. Changing a sentence from a sentence of incarceration to a grant of probation shall constitute a permissible reduction of sentence under this subdivision.

A motion for reduction of sentence is essentially a second opportunity for a defendant to place before the Court the facts relevant to sentencing. *United States v. Colvin*, 644 F.2d 703, 705 (8th Cir. 1981). It also provides a second opportunity for the Court to reconsider its sentence after the passage of a short interval of time and in light of any further information that may be presented to the Court subsequent to sentencing. *Id.*; *United States v. Ellenbogen*, 390 F.2d 537, 5432 (2d Cir.), *cert. denied*, 393 U.S. 918 (1968). It is a plea for leniency, addressed to the sound discretion of the Court. *Poole v. United States*, 250 F.2d 396, 401 (D.C. Cir. 1957). Reduction of a defendant's sentence is appropriate where, upon such reconsideration, the Court finds the sentence to be unduly harsh. *United States v. Colvin*, 644 F.2d 703, 705 (8th Cir. 1981); *United States v. Maynard*, 485 F.2d 247, 248 (9th Cir. 1973).

In ruling on this motion, we request that the Court consider those factors that entered into the original sentencing decision, such as the nature of the offense, the defendant's role in the offense, the defendant's criminal record, and other personal characteristics of the defendant. In addition, with the passage of time since sentencing, this Court may benefit from knowledge of the defendant's adjustment to prison and can better evaluate the facts and arguments presented at sentencing.

As discussed more fully below, the existing conditions of Mrs. Pollard's incarceration provide the Court with a glaring illustration of the severity of her particular sentence. Despite her efforts to adjust to prison life, Mrs. Pollard's rare physical disorders—uncontrollable in a prison setting—subject her to a painful and limited existence. In ruling upon Mrs. Pollard's motion, this Court is asked to acknowledge contemporary standards of decency and humaneness and to release Mrs. Pollard from such harsh punishment.

IV. ARGUMENT

Mrs. Pollard's sentence, as currently imposed, is indeed unduly harsh. The imposition of the full term of incarceration on each count with which Mrs. Pollard was charged represents extremely severe punishment, particularly when that incarceration greatly aggravates Mrs. Pollard's serious medical problems. Moreover, her limited involvement in criminal activity, her complete cooperation with authorities, and her lack of a prior criminal record favor a reduction of her sentence.

A. Reduction Of Sentence Is Necessary Where Mrs. Pollard's Actual Punishment Is Beyond The Justifiable Limits Of Her Sentence.

Regrettably, the fears articulated at Mrs. Pollard's sentencing concerning the treatment of her medical problems in a prison setting have been realized. Notwithstanding incarceration at F.C.I. Lexington, one of the few prison facilities with a medical care unit available to female prisoners, Mrs. Pollard's rare medical condition has not been, and cannot be, treated effectively in prison. Consequently, Mrs. Pollard's incarceration has resulted in additional hardship not suffered by others similarly sentenced. As such, the nature of Mrs. Pollard's incarceration goes beyond the justifiable punishment imposed. *See Battle v. Anderson,* 447 F. Supp. 516, 525 (E.D. Okla.), *aff'd,* 564 F.2d 388 (10th Cir. 1977) ("Persons are sent to prison as punishment, not *for* punishment,").; *Estelle v. Gamble,* 429 U.S. 97, 103 (1976). in *Gamble,* the Supreme Court held that indifference to a prisoner's serious illness stated a cause of action under 42 U.S.C. § 1983 as cruel and unusual punishment forbidden by the Eighth Amendment. In so holding, the Court wrote:

[D]enial of medical care may result in pain and suffering which no one suggests would serve any penological purpose. The infliction of such unnecessary suffering is inconsistent with contemporary standards of decency . . .

429 U.S. at 103 (citations omitted).

Mrs. Pollard has and continues to suffer from several different disorders of her gastro-intestinal tract which require specialized and personal medical treatment. Among other things, Mrs. Pollard has been diagnosed as having gastroparesis, a motor abnormality of the stomach, and biliary dyskinesia, a rare condition resulting from abnormal motility and pressures in the common bile duct.

With respect to the gastroparesis, Mrs. Pollard's stomach has abnormally delayed emptying. As a result, Mrs. Pollard's food, rather than passing out of her stomach through the digestive tract, forms into large, indigestible masses known as bezoars. The bezoars have to be removed or broken up endoscopically[2] so that they can pass through the digestive system. In addition, Mrs. Pollard requires the continuous use of drugs to stimulate the emptying of the stomach.

Compounding this condition, and indeed far more serious, is Mrs. Pollard's biliary dyskinesia condition.[3] Mrs. Pollard was finally diagnosed as having biliary dyskinesia in August of 1986, after having suffered with the condition for a prolonged period of time. Because treatment with medications was unsuccessful, Mrs. Pollard underwent multiple and complex surgery at the University of Illinois in October of 1986. The surgeon, Dr. Robert Baker, removed Mrs. Pollard's gall bladder and enlarged the openings of both her common bile duct and pancreatic duct into the intestinal tract. Although the surgery was designed to reduce pressure and relieve some of Mrs. Pollard's pain, it has not been successful. Clearly, further treatment is needed. However, treatment of this rare disorder is still somewhat experimental and by no means commonly available. It is clearly not available in prison. As a consequence, Mrs. Pollard suffers needlessly, and her incarceration delays treatment of her condition.

Mrs. Pollard's health, poor even before her arrest, has deteriorated significantly. The intense abdominal, chest and back pain, symptomatic of her disorders, have become even more excruciating and debilitating. In addition, Mrs. Pollard continues to endure cramping, burning inflammation of her digestive tract and bouts of nausea and vomiting. As a result, Mrs. Pollard has encountered difficulty in eating or digesting her food properly for any sustained period of time. In fact, since her incarceration at F.C.I. Lexington, Mrs. Pollard often has been put on an all-liquid diet consisting of chicken broth and apple juice by prison doctors. Further, Mrs. Pollard is experiencing frequent headaches, blackouts, general weakness and lassitude.

---

[2]During an endoscopy, a long tube is inserted through the patient's mouth into the digestive tract, allowing a physician to see the internal organs through fiber optics and perform procedures such as biopsies or washing.

[3]Because of the complexity of Mrs. Pollard's condition, she was referred to Dr. Michael Goldberg at the University of Chicago, a specialist in biliary tract disorders, during the summer of 1986.

Due to the combination of these incapacitating symptoms, Mrs. Pollard has been hospitalized for an extended period of time on three separate occasions since arriving at F.C.I. Lexington.[4] The prison doctors have attempted to treat her condition by experimenting with countless numbers of medications. To date, they have been unsuccessful. Indeed, even the painkillers currently prescribed for Mrs. Pollard are only partially effective for limited periods of time.[5] As a result, Mrs. Pollard cannot eat, work or go outside. Mrs. Pollard is under doctor's orders to refrain from working at her assigned dental assistant job. Similarly, doctor's orders prohibit Mrs. Pollard from going outside or from participating in any activities, such as attending educational classes, visiting the library or attending religious services, ostensibly because of her medications. Instead, Mrs. Pollard spends her days and nights literally writhing in pain inside the extended care unit of F.C.I. Lexington. Hence, despite the efforts of doctors at F.C.I. Lexington, Mrs. Pollard continues to endure "pain and suffering which [does not] serve any penological purpose." *Gamble*, 429 U.S. at 703. Consequently, her sentence is effectively enhanced.

Continued incarceration by its very essence will only aggravate Mrs. Pollard's medical condition. First, medical resources at a prison facility, and F.C.I. Lexington in particular, are limited. The facility is serviced by four young and relatively inexperienced doctors who are unable to devote personalized treatment to any one patient. The sheer number of patients to be treated limits and often delays medical treatment. For example, in March of 1987, Mrs. Pollard was informed that an endoscopy and other tests would be conducted to assist the doctors at F.C.I. Lexington in treating her condition. The testing has never been done and after several postponements, Mrs. Pollard is now scheduled to go to the University of Kentucky in July for the tests. Also in March, Mrs. Pollard was informed that a CAT scan would be taken to determine the cause of her headaches. Although she has continued to endure

---

[4] Thus far, Mrs. Pollard has been hospitalized for periods of two weeks and of four to five days. Mrs. Pollard currently is hospitalized and has been for over three weeks.

[5] Among other things, Mrs. Pollard is receiving injections of a painkiller, Nubain, twice a day in an attempt to control her pain. Nubain is frequently used as a surgical anesthetic. According to her former gastroenterologist, the routine use of Nubain is not the optimal therapy for Mrs. Pollard's pain. *See* June 26, 1987 letter from Dr. Herbert A. Moskovitz to James F. Hibey, attached hereto as Exhibit 1.

excruciating headaches, no CAT scan has been taken, and none is presently scheduled. Similarly, the doctors have no expertise in gastrointestinal tract disorders such as those from which Mrs. Pollard suffers and cannot provide Mrs. Pollard with the specialized care her disorders require. Nor will they administer a certain medication which at this time may be the only method available to treat her rare disorder.[6]

Second, Mrs. Pollard's severe pain may in part be attributed to her incarceration. The unanimous opinion of the doctors who have treated Mrs. Pollard—her regular gastroenterologist in Washington, D.C., the specialists to whom he referred her, and her physician at F.C.I. Lexington[7]—is that Mrs. Pollard's enhanced pain is due to the stress which is attendant to her confinement and its effect on her already-weakened medical condition. The doctors suggest that much of this pain is difficult to treat and may not be corrected by surgery or other medication available at the prison. Rather, reduction in Mrs. Pollard's stress level is a key to alleviating her incapacitating pain. Unfortunately, Mrs. Pollard's stress level is high largely due to the fact that she is incarcerated—there can be no more stressful a situation than confinement in prison. Consequently, although Mrs. Pollard is probably receiving as good medical care at Lexington as she could receive at any federal correctional institution,[8] the very state of incarceration produces a condition that the prison hospital is incapable of treating. The result is suffering far greater than that contemplated by a sentence

[6]One bright prospect for the treatment of Mrs. Pollard's condition and the alleviation of some of her pain is the motility-stimulating drug, domperidone (trade name Motilium). The drug, which would allow Mrs. Pollard to digest her food, has not been released for general use in this country by the Food and Drug Administration, although it has been used effectively in Canada and Western Europe to treat motility disorders like Mrs. Pollard's. See Exhibit 1. To date, officials at F.C.I. Lexington and the Bureau of Prisons have refused to approve the use of domperidone in treating Mrs. Pollard because of the lack of FDA approval. See April 13, 1987 letter from Warden R. L. Matthews to James F. Hibey, attached hereto as Exhibit 2; June 1, 1987 letter from Assistant Surgeon General, USPHS to James F. Hibey, attached hereto as Exhibit 3.

[7]Since March 4, 1987, when Mrs. Pollard arrived at F.C.I. Lexington, her medical care has already been successively assigned to three different doctors. The third doctor, apparently new to the institution, was just assigned to Mrs. Pollard's case lask week.

[8]Mrs. Pollard is not suggesting that she could receive better medical care elsewhere in the federal prison system or that she should be transferred to another facility. Rather, she contends that *no* prison medical facility can adequately treat conditions that are either caused or aggravated by the situation of incarceration in the first place.

for a term of years. Thus, not only is Mrs. Pollard's five-year sentence unduly harsh in light of the limited nature of her criminal activity, but five years is even harsher in her case because of the ravaging effects of incarceration on her health.

In contrast, reduction of Mrs. Pollard's sentence will provide her with the opportunity to obtain the specialized and personal medical care required for treatment of her condition. For example, both of Mrs. Pollard's specialists have recommended additional treatment such as undergoing another gastric emptying study and an endoscopic retrograde cholangiopancreatogram. Outside of prison, Mrs. Pollard will be better able to secure such timely treatment which is presently unavailable to her. Indeed, Mrs. Pollard will have the ability to seek out specialists and undergo various methods of treatment at a minimum, she will not be forced to delay for several months treatment and testing—such as an endoscopy or a CAT scan—that are recommended and necessary. Reduction of Mrs. Pollard's sentence provides her with the opportunity for medical treatment beyond mere maintenance of her pain and with the possibility of eating, sleeping and working on a regular basis.

Simply stated, Mrs. Pollard has legitimate health problems which are not being treated in prison. As a result, she cannot eat or function as a normal human being. And it is clear that she cannot live with such pain for the rest of her life. It is imperative that she seek and obtain treatment and relief; but she cannot do so as long as she is incarcerated. She should not be allowed to remain in such a physical condition for the remainder of her sentence. Indeed, her condition could worsen if she does not obtain proper medical care. *See* Exhibit 1. No societal interest is served by requiring Mrs. Pollard effectively to postpone her efforts to obtain the specialized care she needs.

B. *Reduction Of Sentence Is Appropriate Where Mrs. Pollard's Limited Involvement In Her Husband's Activities Does Not Justify Her Harsh Sentence.*

Anne Pollard's case is not Jonathan J. Pollard's case. Though the cases are intertwined, her case in essence and categorically is distinct from that of her husband.

Mrs. Pollard was not a co-conspirator in her husband's admitted espionage on behalf of Israel, nor was she an aider and abettor. She had neither the intent nor the capability of undertaking espionage. She was simply a loving wife who responded to her husband's call for help. While Mrs. Pollard may have more readily justified helping her husband because of her own Zionist sympathies, she did not undertake to remove documents from the Pollard's apartment in order to harm the United States or to aid a foreign government. Her actions were based on the fact that, politics aside, her highest loyalty was to her husband. She chose to support him, right or wrong, out of her love and her felt duty as a wife. It may well have been that loyalty and love, blind to the ramifications of her actions, that lead Mrs. Pollard to her involvement in this case, but she nevertheless has accepted full responsibility for her actions.

Mrs. Pollard has paid the ultimate price for that love—she has suffered through the humiliation and degradation of a criminal prosecution and, most importantly, she has lost her freedom. Moreover, she continuously faces the realization that she has lost her husband to a life sentence and that the resulting prospect of any family life with him or any children is bleak.

Mrs. Pollard is left only with deteriorating health and a marriage in name only. However, she has steadfastly rejected the suggestions of various friends and inmates to consider divorcing her husband. While some have pointed out to Mrs. Pollard that she would not be in federal prison but for her husband, she has refused to blame him for her predicament. Instead, she has been devastated by her separation from him; and she lives for the 15 minutes per month that she can speak to him by telephone. Mrs. Pollard's unwavering love of her husband demonstrates the bona fides of her assertions that she was motivated out of concern for her husband, not out of greed or out of any calculated desire to engage in espionage. For this reason, her case should be viewed in a far different light than an ordinary criminal case.

In negotiating a plea agreement with the prosecution, the defense carefully crafted the plea to describe accurately the limited extent of criminal involvement to which Mrs. Pollard would plead guilty. The plea was intended to make clear that Mrs. Pollard did not commit espionage. She is not a spy, and she should not be punished as one. We submit that she has. Under the circumstances presented herein, the severity of Mrs. Pollard's sentence is not justified.[9]

Furthermore, to a large extent, Mrs. Pollard's experience has already served as a sobering example of the suffering that befalls someone in her situation. She has been arrested, thrown in jail, prosecuted, convicted and sentenced in highly publicized proceedings. The three months she spent in D.C. Jail were a nightmare of poor health, unbearable conditions and isolation, all of which amounted to needless suffering. Her reputation, both personal and professional, is largely ruined. The man she married just three months before her arrest is in prison for life, dashing all hopes for living a normal life together and raising a family. As outlined in more detail above, Mrs. Pollard's health has deteriorated significantly since her arrest, most notably due to incarceration, first in D.C. Jail and currently in F.C.I. Lexington. Under these circumstances, the additional punishment of incarceration in a federal prison for five years is indeed unduly harsh.

C. A Reduction Of Sentence Is Appropriate Where Mrs. Pollard Has Demonstrated Her Cooperation And Good Behavior Since Her Arrest.

Additional considerations warrant a reduction of Mrs. Pollard's sentence. Foremost is her valuable cooperation throughout this case. While the government previously acknowledged the value of Mrs. Pollard's cooperation in this matter,[10] the sentence imposed by the Court does not accord her due credit for that cooperation. Mrs. Pollard initiated her cooperation in this case prior to reaching any plea agreement with the U.S. Attorney's Office. Thereafter, even when experiencing severe pain, she truthfully and com-

---

[9] Mrs. Pollard's sentence is particularly harsh when her actions are compared to those of Sharon Scranage, an American citizen who, according to news reports, passed classified information obtained at her workplace at the Central Intelligence Agency to her Ghanaian boyfriend. The classified information included the identities of covert CIA informants in Ghana. Ms. Scranage was sentenced originally to five years in prison. *See* April 10, 1986 UPI article, attached hereto as Exhibit 4. In contrast, Mrs. Pollard never passed any classified information to any foreign national. Yet, in spite of all other mitigating factors discussed herein, she remains in prison to serve the maximum of five years on each of the counts to which she pleaded guilty.

[10] *See* Government's Memorandum In Aid of Sentencing at pp. 17–18.

prehensively disclosed to the investigators what she knew of her husband's activities and contacts, answering specific questions raised by the authorities and testifying as requested. Now, in the aftermath of sentencing, the impact of Mrs. Pollard's disclosures can more readily be seen. For example, Mrs. Pollard was able to corroborate facts establishing the involvement of certain Israeli nationals in an espionage conspiracy.[11] Even though Mrs. Pollard is not solely responsible for these results, her cooperation is significant and should be valued accordingly. Furthermore, Mrs. Pollard's willingness to cooperate should be recognized as evidence of her forthright and truthful character.

In a broader sense, Mrs. Pollard's cooperative attitude throughout this case—not merely in sharing her knowledge with government investigators, but also in abiding by the conditions of her release prior to sentencing and by the conditions of her plea agreement—should be considered as a mitigating factor justifying a reduction of sentence. Mrs. Pollard amply demonstrated her ability and desire to live a productive, law-abiding life throughout the period following her release from custody. She carefully abided by the many restrictions on her lifestyle while maintaining steady employment.[12] By way of illustration, Mrs. Pollard dutifully reported to the D.C. Pretrial Services Agency by telephone on a daily basis, and in person on a weekly basis. In addition, she adhered to the restrictions prohibiting any travel outside the Washington, D.C. metropolitan area, with limited exceptions including visits to her husband and trips to obtain required medical care. After entering her guilty plea, Mrs. Pollard carefully followed the provisions of her plea agreement as well as those governing her release pending sentence.[13] Furthermore, throughout this period, Mrs. Pollard demonstrated that she poses no danger to the community.[14]

[11] Colonel Aviem Sella, Mr. Pollard's initial "handler," was indicted only days before this Court sentenced Mr. and Mrs. Pollard. In addition, it has been reported that a federal grand jury continues to investigate three of Mr. Pollard's contacts—Rafael Eitan, Joseph Yagur and Irit Erb—as additional putative defendants in Mr. Pollard's case.

[12] Her employment was, however, on occasion interrupted by her meetings with the prosecutors and investigators, by her illness and by the surgery required by her medical condition.

[13] The only exception to total adherence to the plea agreement was Mrs. Pollard's interview on CBS's *60 Minutes* and on Israeli television just prior to sentencing. Mrs. Pollard did not profit from the interviews nor did she divulge any classified information (she did not have any to divulge in any event) to the interviewers.

[14] That Mrs. Pollard has no previous criminal record and is not a violent person also weigh heavily in favor of Mrs. Pollard's release.

While in prison, Mrs. Pollard has continued to follow the various rules and regulations governing her conduct. She has generally adjusted well to F.C.I Lexington despite her serious medical difficulties. In addition, she has acknowledged her willingness to abide by restrictions on her First Amendment rights which are currently in force. Nonetheless, these restrictions, which are unreasonable in the absence of any knowledge by Mrs. Pollard of classified information, further illustrate the harsh conditions of her incarceration. Her access to the outside world is severely restricted in a manner wholly inapplicable to other prisoners.[15]

In short, since her arrest, Mrs. Pollard has consistently demonstrated her desire and ability to abide by the laws of society and the far more restrictive limitations placed on someone in her situation. The fact that, in the mounting panic and desperation preceding sentencing, she unwisely granted interviews should be regarded as the aberration it was. Certainly, she should not be punished further because of those interviews.

Mrs. Pollard fervently desires to live a normal, law-abiding life and has been making every effort since her arrest to achieve that goal. Her actions demonstrate the remorse she feels for ever having broken society's laws. There can be no question that Mrs. Pollard has learned a very sobering lesson from her involvement in this case and that she will never again engage in any form of illegal activity. In light of her grave medical condition, her earnest, honest motivations and her very limited involvement in criminal activity, Mrs. Pollard's sentence is indeed unduly harsh.

D. Because The Parole Process Has Already Been Tainted, The Court Should Act Now To Reduce Mrs. Pollard's Sentence.

As we previously suggested at Mrs. Pollard's sentencing, this is not a case in which the Court could have any assurance that Mrs. Pollard will be released by the Parole Board before the termination of the full term of the sentence. The parole guidelines indicate that Mrs. Pollard will probably serve between 40 and 52 months of her

[15] For example, the list of people with whom Mrs. Pollard may visit in person or converse over the telephone is limited. In addition, all correspondence and telephone calls, except for attorney/client matters are monitored. With respect to correspondence, the monitoring/censoring process frequently delays receipt of the correspondence by more than a month.

five year sentence.[16] Thus, the mechanics of the guidelines ensure that Mrs. Pollard will serve most, if not all, of her sentence, with no hope of an early release on parole.

That conclusion is underscored by the government's recent attempt to influence the Parole Board's decision with inflammatory mischaracterizations of Mrs. Pollard's involvement in criminal activities. In anticipation of Mrs. Pollard's appearance before the Parole Board, the government filed its "Report On Convicted Prisoner By United States Attorney" ("Report") and in it stated in very broad and conclusory terms, for example, that Mrs. Pollard aided and abetted Mr. Pollard in his espionage and participated in his efforts to "undermine[ ] the national security." In short, the government told the Parole Board that Mrs. Pollard was a spy, a fiction not supported by the facts. The government proceeds in its Report to claim that Mrs. Pollard "utilized her husband's services as a thief of classified documents" and that she is responsible for the government's present inability to prosecute certain of the Israeli co-conspirators. These conclusory claims misconstrue the true facts.

The last claim—albeit, a feeble attempt by the government to focus the blame on Mrs. Pollard for its inability presently to prosecute Sella, Eitan, Yagur and Irb—is in the section of the Report which is entitled "Cooperation." In that section, the government takes two sentences briefly to describe Mrs. Pollard's cooperation and a full page (of the entire one and two-third pages in the section which includes a bland introductory paragraph) to accuse Mrs. Pollard wrongfully of "play[ing] dumb" with the FBI/NIS agents and of allowing the Israeli co-conspirators to flee to Israel. Such accusations simply are not true. But more importantly, the Parole Board will be left with the distinct impression that Mrs. Pollard's cooperation was of no value in spite of the government's promise in the Plea Agreement to bring the "nature, extent and value of Mrs. Pollard's testimony and continued cooperation" to the attention of the Parole Board. Plea Agreement, ¶ 4 (c).

It serves no useful purpose in this memorandum to address each

---

[16]For some inexplicable reason, Mrs. Pollard's file at F.C.I. Lexington still indicates that she should serve "100+" months. This error, we believed, was addressed by the probation department prior to sentencing (*see* Carlson memorandum, attached hereto as Exhibit 5), but the correction has not been made as yet in her file. This is particularly significant because it is that file which is ultimately reviewed and considered by the Parole Board.

of the government's gross exaggerations and to rehash the facts which were already discussed in detail in Mrs. Pollard's sentencing memorandum. This Court fully understands the charges to which Mrs. Pollard pleaded guilty and the undisputed facts which support those charges. However, it is useful to bring the government's recent actions to the Court's attention because it is only through this Court that Mrs. Pollard will be released prior to the expiration of the full term of her sentence. Realistically, the government has already sealed her fate with the Parole Board[17] and virtually guaranteed that Mrs. Pollard will serve five years in prison. We request that the Court acknowledge that what the government has done in its Report is unfair and that, under all of the circumstances of this case, five years is an unnecessarily harsh sentence.

IV. CONCLUSION

Mrs. Pollard recognizes the wrongfulness of her actions and is sorry for having engaged in illegal conduct. She begs the Court's forgiveness and asks the Court for leniency in considering her request for a reduction of her sentence.

Mrs. Pollard has now served in excess of seven months in the D.C. Jail and in F.C.I. Lexington. We submit that seven months is sufficient under the circumstances of this case to satisfy the interests of justice and of society in general. She should now be released from prison and given the opportunity to obtain effective medical treatment for her medical problems and to lead a successful, law-abiding life.

For the foregoing reasons, Anne Pollard respectfully requests that the Court reduce her sentence to the time served or suspend the remainder of her sentence of incarceration and substitute a period of probation.

---

[17] Mrs. Pollard was originally scheduled to appear before the Parole Board on June 25, 1987. However, when she reviewed her file for the second time in a week on June 23, she for the first time saw the government's Report. At that point, with no opportunity to respond in writing to the government's scurrilous allegations, Mrs. Pollard requested a postponement of her appearance before the Parole Board.

June 26, 1987

James F. Hibey, Esquire
Verner, Liipfert, Bernhard,
McPherson and Hand,
Chartered
1660 L Street, N.W.
Suite 1000
Washington, D.C. 20036
    Re: Anne Henderson
Pollard

Dear Mr. Hibey:

I have been informed by your office that following Mrs. Pollard's incarceration at a federal correctional institution she continues to have her abdominal and chest pain. She also is unable to eat an adequate, normal diet and has episodes of frequent nausea and vomiting. It has also been pointed out to me that she apparently has not been attended by an experienced specialist in the field of gastroenterology. She apparently also weighs slightly less than 100 pounds and has not regained any of the weight she lost prior to her removal to a federal facility. I also understand that she is receiving parenteral Nubain for the control of her pain.

Mr. Hibey, I would like to restress that Mrs. Pollard suffers a very complex constellation of gastrointestinal problems which, in my opinion, can only be properly addressed by regular attendance by a specialist in gastroenterology. I also feel that Nubain is not an optimal drug in this case because it has a definite incidence of gastrointestinal side effects, as well as being known to cause biliary tract spasm; particularly at the Sphincter of Oddi which may be part of the site of her original biliary dyskinetic problems. At this point in time, I feel that good medical practice would demand that she be definitively restudied with regard to her gastric emptying; the current status of her biliary tract pressures and motility; and the result of the surgery performed by Dr. Baker in 1986 at the University of Illinois. Again, I do not feel, in view of my experience as a gastroenterologist, that a routine use of an injectable analgesic is the optimal therapy for her pain, which is presumably of non-malignant G.I. tract origin.

Notwithstanding her incarceration in a federal correctional institution, I strongly feel, as Mrs. Pollard's prior physician and gastroenterologist, that she deserves medical care consonant with the nature and severity of her gastrointestinal illnesses. She should be allowed access to experienced specialists in these disorders. I feel that she should at least be allowed to return for reevaluation by Drs. Goldberg and Baker who, with prior data and familiarity with Mrs. Pollard, might be able to provide expertise and care more expeditiously to improve her health and relieve her pain. In addition, I would not hesitate to prescribe domperidone, a motility stimulating drug, which might assist Mrs. Pollard with her gastric emptying problem and relieve her symptoms. It is a drug which is awaiting release by the FDA following extensive study in this country and successful use in Canada and Western Europe. This could be obtained on application to the FDA. It is apparent to me from my previous experience with Mrs. Pollard that her condition certainly is not going to improve and could worsen if she does not receive timely gastroenterological management, particularly in regard to her gastric emptying problem and whether the surgical decompression of her biliary tract by Dr. Baker has been successful or whether reoperation is an option to be considered. If Mrs. Pollard is having trouble with nausea and vomiting, the possibility of a gastric bezoar should be considered as this has been a significant recurring problem in the past.

Sincerely,
Herbert A. Moskovitz, M.D.

U.S. Department of Justice
Federal Prison System
Federal Correctional Institution
Lexington, KY 40512

April 13, 1987

Mrs James F. Hibey
Attorney at Law
Verner, Liipfert, Bernhard,
   McPherson and Hand
Suite 1000
1660 L Street, N.W.
Washington, D.C. 20036

Dear Mr. Hibey:

Thank you for your letter of April 2, 1987, concerning Ms. Anne Pollard. You ask that we reconsider our decision of denying her treatment with the drug Motilium.

As you indicate in your letter, the drug has not been approved by the Food and Drug Administration for general use in the United States. Lacking such approval, our institutional physicians cannot approve the administration of the Motilium for Ms. Pollard.

Should, in the future, the drug be approved by FDA, and our physicians believe its use medically indicated, we will consider its use consistent with sound medical practice.

We regret our response cannot be more favorable. Please contact us if there are further questions in this regard.

Sincerely,
R. L. Matthews
Warden

June 1, 1987

Mr. James F. Hibey
Verner, Liipfert, Bernhard,
    McPherson and Hand
Law Offices
Suite 1000
1660 L Street, N.W.
Washington, D.C. 20036

Dear Mr. Hibey:

This is in response to your letter of May 5, 1987, regarding Anne H. Pollard, an inmate at the Federal Correctional Institution, Lexington, Kentucky. Ms. Pollard requested your assistance with obtaining permission from the Federal Bureau of Prisons to use the experimental drug, domperidone, for treatment of her gastrointestinal tract disorder.

Since domperidone is an experimental drug that has not been approved by the Food and Drug Administration for use in the United States, her primary physician at Lexington is investigating the feasibility and benefit this medication would have for Ms. Pollard. Upon completion of his investigation, a decision will be made as to whether she will be provided with the medication.

The Federal Bureau of Prisons has been designated by the U.S. Attorney General the responsibility to care for persons assigned to his custody. Therefore, we cannot permit Ms. Pollard's family to provide the drug, domperidone to her or assume the cost of providing this medication for her.

Sincerely,
    ROBERT L. BRUTSCHE, M.D.
Assistant Surgeon General, USPHS
Medical Director

BULLETIN FROM V.P.I.
SPYING SENTENCE REDUCED

WASHINGTON, April 10 (UPI)—A former C.I.A. employee, Sharon Scranage, convicted of espionage for passing classified information to her Ghanaian boyfriend, has been given a reduced prison sentence and can be released after serving only 18 months, her lawyer said today.

Judge Williams on Wednesday ordered that the sentence he imposed on Miss Scranage in November be reduced to two years from five. He questioned the different treatment given to Miss Scranage and her boyfriend, Michael Soussoudis.

Miss Scranage, a native of Northern Neck, Va., pleaded guilty to disclosing classified information to Mr. Soussoudis, including the identities of covert C.I.A. informants in Ghana. Mr. Soussoudis pleaded no contest to espionage charges and was sentenced to 20 years in prison, but he was exchanged for several Ghanaians in a spy exchange between United States and Ghana.

SUBJECT: UNITED STATES ARMAMENT AND DEFENSE;
TRIALS; ESPIONAGE

ORGANIZATION: CENTRAL INTELLIGENCE AGENCY (CIA)

OFFICE OF THE
PROBATION OFFICER
UNITED STATES DISTRICT COURT
FOR THE DISTRICT OF COLUMBIA
3RD AND CONSTITUTION AVENUE, N.W.
WASHINGTON, D.C. 20001-2866
March 2, 1987

EUGENE WESLEY, JR.
CHIEF PROBATION OFFICER

ARNOLD L. HUNTER
DEPUTY CHIEF PROBATION OFFICER

*MEMORANDUM TO THE HONORABLE CHIEF JUDGE
AUBREY E. ROBINSON, JR.*

RE: POLLARD, Anne L.
Henderson
CC# 86–208

We are submitting this memorandum because a computation of the salient factor score in the Anne Henderson Pollard case is incorrect. We indicated on the presentence report that Anne Pollard would probably serve in excess of 100 months if committed to a federal institution for service of sentence as an adult offender. However, upon further investigation it was determined that Anne Pollard should be graded two categories below the underlying offense of Espionage because she was convicted to Accessory After the Fact. Cathy Pinner with the U.S. Parole Commission provided this information. Therefore, the salient factor score should be corrected to read the following:

Salient Factor Score. Based on the combination of the defendant's estimated salient factor and offense severity scores, it is calculated that the defendant would probably serve between 40 and 52 if committed to a *federal* institution for service of sentence as an adult offender.

It should be emphasized that the guideline figures presented are merely estimates of the months the defendant *may* serve in custody, which are given simply as an aid to the Court. The U.S.

Parole Commission will make its own determination of parole release guidelines if the defendant is committed.

Respectfully submitted,

Richard J. Carlson

U.S. Probation Officer

Telephone #: 535-3183

RJC:cf

APPROVED BY: Supervising U.S. Probation Officer

JONATHAN JAY POLLARD'S MEMORANDUM FOR REDUCTION OF SENTENCE

I. INTRODUCTION

Defendant, Jonathan J. Pollard was sentenced on March 4, 1987 to life imprisonment for violation of the espionage laws. His wife, Ann Henderson-Pollard, was sentenced to concurrent five years sentences which are the subject of a separate motion to reduce.

The reasons for reducing Mr. Pollard's sentence are these:

1. Notwithstanding the volume and nature of the classified information given to the Israeli government, the damage to the United States from his conduct was minimal.

2. No due credit for Mr. Pollard's cooperation has been expressed by the government; therefore its commitment to do so in aid of the court's sentencing was breached.

3. The failure to recognize this cooperation through the imposition of a sentence of less than life imprisonment may constitute a precedent in espionage law enforcement that might satisfy visceral reactions to this crime but will make it all the more difficult to obtain full cooperation from suspects in the future cases of espionage prosecuted by the Justice Department.

4. Current standards of sentencing suggest that the present sentence is excessive.

II. ARGUMENT

A. *Damage*

We have stated in one memorandum in aid of sentencing that the damage to the national security resulting from Mr. Pollard's conduct was minimal to the point of being almost non-existent. This contention is extraordinary (although the government has described it otherwise), but true nevertheless. The information here was passed, in violation of the law, to one of our closest allies. There is no evidence of its being or having been further compromised. In Secretary Weinberger's affidavit the damage to our national security was claimed in bureaucratic terms and no evidence was adduced in the record (public or sealed) that persons and/or systems have been compromised by virtue of Mr. Pollard's conduct.

This makes Secretary Weinberger's affidavits particularly shrill and inflammatory. In the first place, his principal affidavit was sealed in its entirety. Yet, Mr. Pollard's response thereto, citing liberally to it, is virtually free of censorship. Secondly, the Secretary's second affidavit, the one that describes Mr. Pollard's conduct as treasonous, is, in its entirety, unclassified. This latter document adds nothing but rank hyperbole. After the sentencing, taking refuge in his classified affidavit, the Secretary claims that Mr. Pollard's lawyers deliberately misrepresented certain of his statements in that affidavit. See Reuters News Service article, dated March 5, 1987, attached hereto as Exhibit B. These kind [sic] of statements are a "forked tongue," representing nothing more than an effort to appeal to one reader or audience to the exclusion of another.[1]

Moreover, others have begun to voice a perception that Secretary Weinberger has a penchant to exaggerate the damage resulting from acts of espionage. Most recently, Secretary Weinberger's claims of severe repercussions to the national security resulting from the clandestine activities of the marines stationed at the U.S. embassy in Moscow have been questioned. See Washington Post article, dated June 16, 1987, attached hereto as Exhibit G. As in Mr. Pollard's case, Mr. Weinberger speaks of damage before the full facts are known.[2]

---

[1] Secretary Weinberger has long been on record as opposed to broader sharing of intelligence with Israel. See New York Times article, dated March 19, 1983. For example, after Israel experienced enormous success in defeating Syrian military forces during its invasion of Lebanon, it offered to share its military strategies with the U.S., as part of an overall intelligence-sharing agreement. Although Israel has over two dozen intelligence-sharing arrangements with the United States, Secretary Weinberger demurred, fearing the long-term commitments of such an agreement. See New York Times article, dated February 10, 1983. Richelson, The "U.S. Intelligence Community" 205 (1985). Only after Congress exerted pressure on Secretary Weinberger did he offer a counter-proposal. See New York Times article, dated March 13, 1983. This undoubtedly accounts for his heavy-handed assessment of the security breaches in this case.

[2] In Secretary Weinberger's defense, it appears that others within the government are not immune from the urge to overstate the damage resulting from acts of espionage. A commentator, comparing the claims of damage made by prosecutors and Defense Department officials in various espionage cases, noted that "in the otherwise publicity-shy world of espionage, superlatives are everywhere." Shenon, "Washington Talk: Cloak and Dagger and Exaggeration," N.Y. Times, February 20, 1987.

It is, therefore, Mr. Pollard's contention that the nature and extent of any injury to the United States from his conduct has yet to be assessed accurately. The inquiry is a valid one: positing the most sensitive item of information the court can recall was given to the Israeli government, how did it harm the national security? True, the Israelis were not supposed to have the information; but that can be said of even the least sensitive of the information passed. Accordingly, the question must be pressed further in order to ascertain the severity of the offense. Nothing in Secretary Weinberger's affidavits even remotely suggests that with the passage of this most sensitive information, there was a loss of systems or personnel or setback of ongoing operations as a result of Mr. Pollard's conduct. Indeed, this recognition is inherent in the decision of the government not to seek life imprisonment for Mr. Pollard.

B. COOPERATION

The way in which the government chose to advocate its position on damage to the national security presaged its barely perceptible statements regarding Mr. Pollard's cooperation in the government's investigation.

The government agreed to set forth in detail the nature, extent and value of Mr. Pollard's cooperation. On many times we received assurances that although a substantial (but not life) sentence would be sought, there would be a full statement regarding Mr. Pollard's cooperation. None was forthcoming. The government's pleadings contained fully two lines of reference to his cooperation and, at allocution, the government belittled the defendant's own efforts, made ir good faith, to identify the areas where he was helpful to the investigation, and contradicted his rendition of the value of his cooperation.

The irony of the government indicting Mr. Pollard's first Israeli contact on the basis of evidence *he alone provided* is all too bitter: the day before Mr. Pollard is sentenced, his testimony before the grand jury, prepared and elicited by the prosecutor, and the sole basis for a criminal charge, is credited as truthful as to each element of the crime of espionage and an Israeli officer is indicted. The next day Mr. Pollard has no credibility at all; he is no longer of value to the government.

It may be that this court would have sentenced Mr. Pollard to life even if the government had been candid in its appraisal of his cooperation; but, certainly, the government's failure to honor its word to him on the critical question of his cooperation certainly sealed his fate. There was no counterpoint to the perception of Mr. Pollard's arrogance.

There was no verification of his good faith in this case. There was no context which the government alone could have supplied that would have allowed for a perspective that an initially-perceived arrogance was in truth an inaccurate picture of the man.

As a remedy for its failure to recognize the value of Mr. Pollard's cooperation, and consistent with its pledge under the plea agreement not to seek a life sentence for Mr. Pollard, the government should not oppose this motion for reduction.[3] Nevertheless, and perhaps not surprisingly, counsel has been informed that an opposition will be forthcoming.

The government undoubtedly will assert that Mr. Pollard's post-plea conduct, specifically his conversations with a reporter and his letter in the *Jewish Advocate* (albeit published without his approval), justifies its filing of an opposition. While Mr. Pollard's conversations with the press were ill-advised, it is interesting that the government took no action to stop them until after sentencing. Even though Mr. Pollard spoke to the press in November, 1986, resulting in disclosures which the government claimed came perilously close to revealing classified information, the government still permitted Mr. Pollard full access to reporters. Only after the court imposed a life sentence did the government exercise its powers to cut off all access by the press to Mr. Pollard and to begin monitoring and censoring his mail. Under the circumstances, these types of communications have been stopped and are no longer a security concern to the government. There is no reason why they should be a factor militating in favor of a maximum sentence.

C. Precedent

There should be concern about the fact that a cooperative de-

---

[3]Immediately after the court imposed sentence on Mr. Pollard, the U.S. Attorney himself, in response to questions regarding the amount of time Mr. Pollard would actually serve, stated that Mr. Pollard will "never see the light of day." *See* Reuters article, dated March 5, 1987. Such statements indicate that the government will, in spite of the plea bargain, attempt to keep Mr. Pollard incarcerated for his entire life.

fendant, for whom it agreed to request a substantial, but not a life sentence, receives nevertheless, a life sentence. In the context of an opposition to the reduction of a sentence, it is a virtual certainty that the government will not own up to this concern. Under such circumstances, it is appropriate for this court to understand that the ramification of its sentence in this case is to chill the prospect of a suspect in another espionage case being willing to cooperate when he knows that it will not affect his sentence at all.

This could have serious repercussions in cases far more serious than this one. For example, a delay in cooperation because the suspect has trouble crediting the government's representations could result in a loss of intelligence systems as well as the lives of intelligence agents. Of course, the government could say that it will simply rely on the ability of its prosecutors to persuade the next spy it uncovers that their word is good; but that is too facile. When any espionage is uncovered, time is of the essence and even the ablest prosecutor will not know how exquisite the time factor is.

Therefore, even if the government will want the maximum sentence to be upheld, this court may, nevertheless, see the wisdom in a reduction in a case such as this where the defendant's cooperation has been complete and valuable to the United States.

D. *Excessiveness*

One trait that the judicial system has striven to exhibit is consistency in sentences for similar crimes. Indeed, the court is required to take into account, when imposing sentence on a defendant, sentences dispensed in similar cases. 18 U.S.C. § 3553(a) states that a court "shall consider . . . (6) the need to avoid unwarranted sentence disparities among defendants with similar records who have been found guilty of similar conduct." In keeping faith with the principle of uniformity, the court should consider whether the sentence given Mr. Pollard far exceeds the terms set by other judges in other cases.

If Mr. Pollard had engaged in espionage for the Soviet Union or an East Bloc country, a life sentence possibly would have comported with other decisions. In recent cases, John Walker, Thomas Cavanagh and Ronald Pelton all received life sentences for passing, or attempting to pass, sensitive national secrets to the Soviets. *See New York Times* articles, dated November 8, 1986, May 25, 1985, and December 17, 1986, Richard Miller received two concurrent life terms plus 50 years for conspiring to pass information to the Soviets while an employee of the FBI, *see New York Times* article, dated July 20, 1986, and a judge sentenced Jerry Whitworth to 365 years for his role in the infamous Walker spy ring. *See New York Times* article, dated August 29, 1986.

Yet, not even those acting to benefit the Soviets necessarily receive lengthy sentences. Two years ago, Samuel Loring Morison, one of Mr. Pollard's co-workers, was convicted of passing a highly classified satellite photo to *Jane's Defense Weekly,* a British publication. In spite of testimony that the publication of the photo gave the Soviet Union a far greater knowledge of U.S. satellite capabilities, the judge sentenced Mr. Morison to only two years in prison. *See New York Times* article, dated December 8, 1985. In 1981 David Barnett was sentenced to 18 years for passing information to the Soviets on U.S. intelligence operations, including the names of dozens of U.S. operatives. *See New York Times* article, dated June 29, 1981. William Holden Bell received a sentence of 8 years for his role in providing information on antitank missile and radar technology to a Polish agent. *Id.; see New York Times* article, dated December 17, 1981. In 1984 a judge in Florida sentenced Ernst Forbrich to 15 years for purchasing U.S. military secrets with the intent of passing them to East Germany. *See New York Times* article, dated August 4, 1984. Svetlana Ogorodnikova, a Soviet emigree, received 18 years in 1985 for conspiring with Richard Miller to deliver classified documents to the Soviet Union. *See New York Times* article, dated July 16, 1985,

In vivid contrast, persons acting on behalf of non-Soviet countries have received far lesser sentences. For example, Enseign [sic] Stephen Baba was court-martialed for having sent documents relating to electronic warfare secrets and indices of code words to the South African embassy. The court imposed a sentence of eight years at hard labor, yet under a plea bargain the sentence was reduced to two years. *See New York Times* articles, dated December, 4, 1981, December 18, 1981, and January 21, 1982. Similarly, Sharon Scranage gave her boyfriend, a Ghana national, information gained as a CIA employee relating to the names of CIA operatives in Ghana. Though the information could have resulted in the loss of lives of several operatives, the court sentenced Ms. Scranage to five years. Shortly thereafter, the court reduced the sentence to two years. *See New York Times* article, dated April 11, 1986. In both cases, the nation receiving the information was not considered an ally of the United States. Indeed, neither country even had particularly friendly relations with the United States. Nevertheless, the judges presumably viewed the fact that the classified information was not passed to the Soviet Union as a relevant factor in sentencing.

Viewed in the context of other cases, Mr. Pollard's sentence is excessive. Espionage on behalf of one of the United States' closest allies does not merit the maximum sentence, especially in light of Mr. Pollard's guilty plea and cooperation, and the implicit recognition by the government, in the form of its agreement not to seek a life term, that the damage to the national security was not as great as Secretary Weinberger would have the court believe.

LETTER FROM JONATHAN POLLARD TO ROBERT COHN (ROBERT COHN IS EDITOR OF *ST. LOUIS JEWISH LIGHT*)

Springfield, MO
June 29, 1987
2 Tammuz 5741

Dear Mr. Cohn,

Although I have long debated about whether or not I should write to you, something I read in the newspaper today decided the issue for me. The Administration's recently announced plan to grant Egypt co-production rights for the M1, the army's top-of-the-line main battle tank, seemed to confirm all my worst fears about the true nature of Mr. Weinberger's Middle East agenda. In many respects, this tank deal seems emblematic of his notorious "even-handedness" policy for the region, which, over the course of five long years, I had the dubious honor of watching unfold before my eyes. Indeed, it was my implacable opposition to this policy which eventually precipitated my involvement with Israelis.

Stripped of its Cold War camouflage, the Weinberger doctrine hopes to keep Israel on the strategic defensive by creating a more "equitable" balance of power between her and the surrounding Arab states. While some people are slowly recognizing the fact that this policy has been the motive force behind Mr. Weinberger's indefatigable championing of increased arms sales to such "moderate" Arab countries as Saudi Arabia, Jordan and Egypt, what has gone largely unnoticed, however, has been his parallel attempt to severely restrict the flow of vital intelligence to Israel. In addition to significantly enhancing the effectiveness of all the new Eastern Bloc military equipment currently passing into the armories of Syria, Iraq and Libya, this little known, undeclared intelligence embargo is also intended to deny Israel the type of information needed for her to undertake diplomatically controversial but militarily essential operations against a whole spectrum of targets ranging from distant terrorist bases, like the PLO headquarters in Tunis, to others which one day might pose a direct threat to the very survival of the Jewish state. In Mr. Weinberger's opinion, though, by restraining Israel's "irresponsibly" aggressive behavior towards her neighbors, his policy would facilitate a new era in United States-Arab relations. There are, of course, other implications of Mr. Weinberger's geopolitical initiative which are not so "positive."

In the event this policy was successfully implemented and a situation analogous to June 1967 were to reoccur, it is assumed that Israel would probably be unable to launch a cost effective conventional preemptive strike against the Arab armies massing along her frontier. Israel's decision makers would therefore be left in the unenviable position of having to choose between "a ruinous war or a shameful peace," which is precisely the type of excruciating dilemma that Mr. Weinberger feels would make them more receptive to "legitimate" Arab political grievances. What is clearly apparent, then, is that Mr. Weinberger's objective of creating a so-called "level battlefield" in the region would, if realized, eliminate the Israeli army's military superiority over the Arabs which has traditionally served to deter the more belligerent elements within their camp.

If seen within this context, the significance of the proposed M1 deal cannot be overemphasized since it would finally provide Egypt with the means by which she could rapidly remilitarize Sinai—and that, Mr. Cohn, is a certain eventuality as far as the Egyptian General Staff is concerned. Apart from nature's abhorrence of a vacuum, the Egyptian officer corps firmly believes that it was robbed of its victory in 1973 by being diplomatically prevented from reoccupying the entire Sinai Peninsula in force. This position hardly represents the views of a disgruntled, extremist faction within the military elite since Egyptian strategic policy has traditionally stressed that the country's first line of defense should run from Gaza to Beersheba and that the Negev, abandoned in 1984, is the territorial avenue through which Egypt can manifest her rightful role in the Arab world. However, balancing this exaggerated sense of injured national pride is the rather sober realization that until the Egyptian army replaces all of its old Soviet supplied

equipment with up-to-date American or European arms, it will be
unable to assert what it considers to be its legitimate rights in Sinai.
Although Mr. Weinberger is fully aware of this revanchist senti-
ment, he has, nevertheless, done everything in his power to satisfy
even the most extreme and unjustified Egyptian request for arms
since he regards the creation of a completely modernized Egyptian
military establishment as the basis of a new regional balance between Israel and Syria: i.e. it is hoped that a greatly improved
Egyptian army would pose such a latent threat to the Negev that
the Israelis would be prevented from conducting the type of overwhelming force necessary to crush Syria in a short, decisive campaign comparable to her stunning 1982 victory.

These types of lop sided Israeli victories are particularly galling to
Saudi Arabia, which views them as an insult to Arab honor, a cause
of Arab political radicalism, and an open invitation for further
Soviet meddling in the area. Mr. Weinberger evidently shares this
warped perspective and avidly backs the contention that peace will
prevail as long as Israel is militarily stymied. Bearing in mind,
though, the Soviet Union's publicly articulated pledge to guarantee
the principle of Syrian strategic "parity" with Israel, it is not entirely clear how Mr. Weinberger's intended hobbling of the Israeli
army could possibly serve to curb either Mr. Assad's territorial
ambitions in Lebanon or his long sought dream of reconquering
the Golan Heights by force of arms.

The only way to resolve this apparent flaw in Mr. Weinberger's
policy is to see the issue of war and peace through Saudi eyes since
they have largely shaped the Secretary's highly skewed appreciation of Middle East political dynamics. According to Riyadh, the
real threat to regional stability is posed by Israel's "reckless" abuse
of her military superiority, which in turn has permitted the Russians to gain a foothold in the area as a needed counterweight. As
far as the Saudis are concerned, then, the only way to safeguard
continued western access to Middle East oil is to replace the much
overrated United States-Israeli special relationship with an alternative strategic alignment with the Arabs, which would be predi-
cated, in part, upon a de facto Pax Syriana [sic] over Lebanon and
an Arab ability to coerce Israel into evaluating all the lands she
occupied during the Six Day War—including, it should be noted,
Jerusalem and the Golan Heights. While the Saudis seem resigned

to the fact that Israel probably has the ultimate means of assuring her own existence, they are, nevertheless, absolutely determined to reduce her to a more "acceptable" size one way or another. Central to this Saudi agenda is the American recognition of Israel's marginal value as a strategic asset and political ally. That Mr. Weinberger has indeed approved such a radical pro-Arab tilt in United States Middle East policy can be readily discerned by his decisions to provide the "moderate" Arab states with virtually unlimited amounts of ultra-sophisticated arms; to deny Israel critical information needed to neutralize the new generation of Soviet weapons being deployed along her northern border; to brand Israel the aggressor in the Lebanon war; and to lobby vigorously for the imposition of punitive arms sanctions upon her; to dilute the importance of Israel's major non-NATO ally status by confirming a similar honor upon Egypt; to tacitly condone the development of Arab unconventional weapons systems which one day will threaten Israeli population centers; and to relegate Israel to a position of strategic irrelevance by dramatically committing the United States to an active defense of Arab political interests in the Persian Gulf War. Taken collectively, these initiatives completely undermine the solemn pledge given by President Reagan to Menachem Begin following the evacuation of Yamit that the United States would guarantee Israel's continued military superiority over the Arabs. Congressional efforts to honor this commitment, however, should not in any way obscure Mr. Weinberger's resolute opposition to it.

Clearly, whatever else can be said about Weinberger's "evenhandedness" policy, it does not bode very well for the long-term security of the Jewish state. It certainly does nothing to deter the Arabs from attempting to take advantage of their new found military strength should relations with Israel significantly deteriorate in the future. At the very least this could result in their adoption of a coordinated war plan similar to the one which inflicted grievous losses upon Israel in 1973. It must be kept in mind, though, that given the relentless effort which is being made by Secretary of Defense Weinberger to prevent Israel from adequately assessing the nature of the potential threat she faces, the carnage of the Yom Kippur War could actually pale in comparison to the next conflict. As Mr. Weinberger is undoubtedly aware of the fact that accurate and timely intelligence is the sine quo non [sic] of Israel's ability to effectively defend herself from the dangers posed by unpredictable and unprincipled neighbors, his policy is nothing short of cold blooded treachery.

Having finally come to the realization that no member of the American Jewish establishment would ever believe that this particular administration would countenance such a duplicitous policy, I agreed to help Israel circumvent Mr. Weinberger's intelligence embargo. But before you rush to pass judgment on the propriety of my actions, Mr. Cohn, tell me what you would have done if you were in my situation? Go to the press and run the risk of having sensitive information inadvertently leaked to the Russians? Turn your eyes away from what was going on and try to live with the potential consequences? Convince yourself that the security of three million hard pressed Jews was worth less than your loyalty to a man [sic] pledged to destroy them? After months of agonizing over this dilemma, I came to the conclusion that the choice I faced was between my belief in Israel's right to continued security and my legal obligation to uphold Mr. Weinberger's betrayal of the Jewish state. Having thus identified my options, I acted accordingly.

Although I am deeply sorry that I had to break the law in order to provide information to Israel that should have been made available in any event, I at no time considered what I was doing to be directed against the United States. How could it be? Both Israel and the United States are sister democracies, share a common cultural heritage, and are, at least in the opinion of some people, close allies which are united in their resolute opposition to the further spread of communism. Unfortunately, as long as the American Jewish community is willing to accept Draconian sentences with equanimity, then it must also accept the twisted political premise which justified them: namely, that an "overly strong" Israel is somehow inimical to American strategic interests in the Middle East. It should be clearly understood that Jewish acquiescence in this matter will have far reaching repercussions since it will, in effect, endorse Weinberger's malevolent attempt to judicially recast the image of Israel as a military and political liability for this country. Indeed, if Weinberger's ultimate goal is to place Israel at the mercy of the Arabs, then this artfully manipulated case has demonstrated the Jewish community's apparent indifference to the maintenance of a strong, democratic national homeland in the

Middle East. My wife and I were not on trial, Mr. Cohn, Israel was and she was ill-served by her Diaspora children when they chose to run away from Mr. Weinberger's indirect assault upon their territorial inheritance.

Although I was somewhat prepared for the near pathological behavior exhibited towards us by certain high ranking members of the present administration, who have never made a secret of their animosity to the state of Israel, I have been utterly devastated by the disgraceful reaction of some otherwise "respectable" Jewish leaders to our plight. From my perspective, their unseemly equivocation on the issue of a Jew's unconditional responsibility to help ensure the survival of Israel is the hidden tragedy of this affair since they are calling into question a fundamental of our faith: namely, that the welfare of the Jewish people comes before *anything* else—even one's own personal security. To be honest with you, Mr. Cohn, I had never really understood the meaning of the term "Kaiserjuden" [sic] or court Jew until I read that Morris Abram had literally rejoiced in Jerusalem over our totally unjustified sentences. It was at that point that the specter of Gedaliah rose before my eyes and the ominous prophecy of Yeshayahu seemed confirmed: "Those who would overthrow you, and those who would destroy you, come from your midst."

Having been involved with several abortive efforts on behalf of the Falashas long before it was "fashionable" to recognize the legitimacy of their heritage, I've been painfully aware of the fact that a depressing number of our self-appointed Jewish leaders here in the United States can be incredibly evasive whenever they are asked to take risks which might jeopardize their carefully manicured reputations as stalwart members of American society. Since their concept of Zionism doesn't extend beyond their pocket books and lavishly organized fund raising galas, they are incapable of appreciating those instances in which a Diaspora Jew may have to put everything on the line in order to safeguard the security of Israel. Do they have such selective memories that they've already forgotten the incredible sacrifices made by a handful of American Jews who, during the 1948 War of Independence, either violated countless criminal statutes by smuggling munitions to Israel or risked losing their United States citizenship by actually fighting for the Jewish state? Were these individuals traitors too? Applying the rather self-serving code of propriety advocated by Morris Abram, men like my uncle, who as an army doctor illegally diverted tons of medicine to help save Israeli wounded and Rudolf Sonneborn, the wealthy industrialist responsible for having organized a covert arms purchasing network in this country for the Hagana, should have been disowned by the Jewish community and thrown in jail. As far as I'm concerned *they* represent everything that is good and noble in American Jewry, whereas Mr. Abram appears to be nothing more than a petty opportunist who craves his role as the community's political watchdog.

As incomprehensible as it may seem, one of the greatest obstacles that must be overcome in the process of solidifying the living bond which unites the Diaspora and Israel is the resistance of some local Jews who are evidently so concerned that such trans-national allegiance to a "foreign" country may call into question their standing in the American political hierarchy that they become, to paraphrase Chaim Weizmann, 105% American and by doing so bring the very suspicion upon themselves they'd hoped to avoid. Although cynics might take cold comfort in the thought that this obsession with maintaining a "proper" distance from Israel is merely a tactical concession to the inexplicable insularity of American culture, it would be more accurate to say that our overly self-conscious brethren have simply booked first-class passage aboard the proverbial ship of fools. Indeed, the uncritical faith with which these hyper assimilationists take for granted their own security in this country is sadly reminiscent of the Jewish grandees of medieval Spain and Portugal who never could have imagined that the ninth of Av would one day come to memorialize their own collective destruction—but it did.

As such tragedies are the indisputable hallmark of our people's long and disappointing exile, it would be the height of self-deception for the American Jewish community to blithely assume that it will somehow escape the ineluctable laws of probability. Of course, there are some essentially "Hellenized" Jews who refuse to acknowledge the Diaspora's continued vulnerability and believe that Israel has been essentially supplanted by the United States as a "safe" alternative promised land—a second Jerusalem if you will. This is a view which parallels in many respects the discredited notions of that archetypal anti-Zionist Lucien Wolf, who nearly sacrificed the embryonic Third Jewish Commonwealth on the altar of his Edwardian Anglophilia. As I recall it, Wolf's view was that western Jews by virtue of their emancipation had no reason (i.e. right) to embrace a separate Jewish nationalism which might alienate them from their fellow countrymen: western Jews were simply Frenchmen or Englishmen who happened to be of the Jewish faith. Personally, I find these "accidental" Jews to be anathema and an insult to the countless generations of our forefathers who underwent 2,000 years of martyrdom forever praying to see the restoration of Zion as an independent Jewish homeland. The United States is a fantastic country, Mr. Cohn, but as wonderful as it appears to be, we should never lose sight of the fact that it, like Mr. Wolf's England, is still only an outpost of the Jewish race and not a substitute for Israel. Unfortunately, it would seem that such convictions have now become seditious and an embarrassment for our image sensitive co-religionists who evidently prefer to espouse a more tentative view of Israel's relevance to upward mobile American Jews. Somehow these "emancipated" Jews have forgotten that Jewish nationalism and faith are identical and that they are both being threatened now by the Scylla of western nationalism and the Charybdis of Arab belligerency.

Whatever else can be said about my case, it has certainly underscored the almost primal fear of racial stigmatization that literally permeates some august members of our Jewish community. Emblematic of these "fair weather" Zionists is Morris Abram, who had the audacity to melodramatically condemn my loyalty to Israel as a threat to the very existence of the Jewish establishment in this country, as if such partiality to one necessarily worked to the detriment of the other. This line of reasoning is nothing short of casuistry and suggests to me that Abram has foresworn his absolute racial obligation to do whatever is required to protect Jewish lives which are threatened. There is an emotive song of the Jewish partisans of World War II that these timid Jews should always keep in mind whenever they rush to repudiate me: "If I am not for myself, who will be for me? If not this way, how? If not now, when?" I ask you, Mr. Cohn, have the fires of the concentration camps grown so cold that people have forgotten how close we came to extinction while the whole world looked away with studied indifference? Has the carnage of the Neve Shalom Synagogue in Istanbul grown so commonplace that people have forgotten that we are still considered fair game for slaughter? Have the burial ceremonies at the military graveyards in Israel grown so heroic that people have forgotten the grim price of independence? Creatures of the night like Morris Abram and William Safire, a pompous pseudo-Zionist if ever there were one, should remember these scenes before they fling themselves at the feet of Chmelnizki's descendent in the Pentagon and relegate me to the status of an aberration. I am not. Experience has taught us that the only laws we should follow unquestioningly are those pertaining to the covenant and survival. I realize that it's a dirty, sordid business at times, but what alternative do we have? Trust Mr. Weinberger and bear silent witness to yet another Holocaust of our people? Perhaps Morris Abram and his ilk should just limit themselves to fund raising and leave the less glamourous [sic] affairs such as intelligence gathering to those of us who are not afraid to be exposed as "unhyphenated" Jews. But these glib apologists, mesmerized by the "Goldine Medina," have self-indulgency [sic] declared the millennia while still in the depths of Galut, as Shlomo Avineri charged, and expect everyone to forget that our war of survival is *still* raging unabated. I think these are the people who Weizmann had in mind when he coined the phrase "the tragedy of the emancipated Jew."

It is incredible to say this but if Mr. Abram had actually bothered to read my indictment, he would have seen that I was only charged with having assisted the state of Israel—*not* a belligerent, *not* with the intent of harming the United States, and certainly *not* for monetary gain. Contrary to all the manure spread about by the U.S. Attorney, I never asked the Israelis for anything during the first six months of the operation which is a fact that has been conveniently overlooked by everyone. The issue of money was first raised when I was told that I would have to go to Europe to meet my Israeli control officer, Rafi Eitan. I wasn't given tickets to go overseas, Mr. Cohn, but was expected to pay for them up front out of my own pocket in the expectation of being reimbursed at some later date. As a result, my wife and I were left with a $5,000 American Express debt that we were asked to take care of ourselves so as not to encumber Israeli funds needed elsewhere. It sounds like I had a wonderful deal, right? When we travelled through Europe, we had to follow an itinerary established by the Israeli security officers: admittedly some hotels were five star, because those were where I had business to conduct; some were the equivalent of Holiday Inns; others were the type that respectable people generally don't patronize; and yes, there were several occasions where my wife and

I had to pull over and sleep in the car so our movements couldn't be traced through hotel receipts. These were the same trips, by the way, which were disingenuously described by the U.S. Attorney as the height of "sybaritic extravagance." No doubt the hotel we stayed in in Pisa would be happy to know that its cold water broom closets are being held in such high esteem by the government prosecutor. We lived in a modest rented apartment and drove a non descript seven year old car, which is not the type of life style that one would expect from venal "turn coats" out to peddle intelligence to the highest bidder. My lord, if I were a mercenary, I should have sold Israeli secrets to the Arabs, who would have been only too happy to pay a fortune for them. What a lot of people simply don't understand is that this was a rather sophisticated affair, logistically speaking, and that I was responsible for paying certain recurrent bills which were generated as a direct result of my involvement with the Israelis. For example, I recruited and was then obliged to subsidize a Saudi bureaucrat who soaked up tons of money in the process of assuaging his guilt. At our sentencing, the United States Attorney played up an expensive dinner I hosted while failing to mention the fact that the only people in attendance were Israeli members of the team who I was expected to entertain while they were in Washington. The way it was presented in court, it sounded like the dinner in question was a standard every day affair for my wife and me. And as far as the secret Swiss bank account was concerned, I never asked for this and was told that it was essentially for the team's use and that I would only be able to access it in order to meet operational expenses.

You should understand, Mr. Cohn, that the present administration had its own warped political agenda in this case that would not have been well served by prosecuting an ideologue who took pains to avoid compromising any American military or diplomatic secrets. Contrary to what Mr. Reagan has evidently been told, *none* of the material made available to the Israelis had anything to do with either American codes, encryption technology, military equipment, strategic warfare plans and capabilities, troop deployments, or the names and locations of covert agents. In Secretary Weinberger's affidavit, the "damage" to national security was claimed in lame bureaucratic terms (i.e. a temporary loss of negotiating advantage) and no evidence was adduced in the record (public or sealed) that persons and/or systems had been compromised by my conduct.

None. I was tasked very carefully, Mr. Cohn, to respect my collection activities to matters pertaining to Arab military capabilities, current and projected Russian technology, and terrorist movements. And far from being a security risk, Israel has a much better track record of protecting sensitive United States intelligence shared with her than some of our NATO allies, such as Great Britain and West Germany. So where is the untold damage to the national defense that Mr. Reagan rather carelessly alluded to in his interview with the *St. Louis Jewish Light?* It would seem that he knows about as much information concerning my activities as he claims to know about the workings of his own National Security Council.

Regretfully, the government's uncomplimentary portrayal of my motives in this affair was initially provided by certain Israelis who evidently found it more expedient to repudiate a so-called "mercenary" than to explain why a Jewish agent had been casually discarded during the course of an officially sanctioned high risk operation. Despite the fact that this utter misrepresentation of my intentions was subsequently refuted, the Justice Department, which has long been regarded as being antagonistic to Israel, found it quite useful to maintain the fiction of my venality in order to place the operation and me in the worst possible light. I need not remind you, Mr. Cohn, that in this type of murky affair, by blackening the moral character of an agent, one suddenly discredits his cause as well—and that was the whole objective of this carefully orchestrated judicial farce.

I don't know whether you're aware of this fact or not, but shortly after my sentence was imposed, certain elements within the Justice and Defense Departments tried to have Israel placed on the "Critical Country List," which would have categorized her with such pariah states as Lybia [sic], Cuba, and North Korea. Had this been accomplished, the American Zionist movement would have ben classified as a subversive ideological threat, equivalent to communism and Islamic extremism, the tax deductibility of donations to Zionist organizations would in all likelihood have been lifted, leading personalities of the movement would have been subjected to intensive surveillance, and severe export controls would have been applied to sophisticated military arms sales to Israel. Although the Arabists in Washington ultimately failed in their attempt to use my case as a means of realizing this particular hidden sentencing agenda, it was certainly not for want of trying.

In spite of the fact that the so called "independent" court was presented with overwhelming evidence substantiating the lack of damage to American security by my actions, Mr. Weinberger apparently stimulated by an eleventh hour visit by Prince Bandar, the Saudi Ambassador in Washington, submitted a now infamous private denunciation of me to the judge in which it was claimed that, by ensuring Israel's continued military superiority over the Arabs, I had irretrievably damaged American defense interests, contributed to instability in the Middle East and weakened America's standing in the Arab world. Needless to say, this inane polemic lacked any legal merit and constituted nothing more than a transparent attempt to help the Administration rebuild its credibility with the Arabs, which had been severely tarnished by the Iranian arms scandal. But perhaps most distressing of all, though, was that by endorsing Caspar Weinberger's rather fanciful off-the-record assessment of my actions as having constituted "the gravest assault against the integrity of this country's national defenses in over two hundred years," Mr. Abram had unwittingly abetted the pernicious Saudi claim that Israel represented as much of a threat to the United States as did the Soviet Union. This is a patently absurd contention which should have been immediately flung back in Weinberger's face by the American Jewish political establishment—irrespective of what it might have thought about me. Moreover, the fact that the present Adminsitration had originally violated the unwritten understanding with Israel not to recruit each other's citizens as agents, was purposely withholding critical information from Israel which it had pledged in good faith to provide her and has been pursuing this case in the most inflammatory manner possible represent concerns that are at least as important to address as was the "impropriety" of Israel operating an agent within (not *against*) the United States intelligence community. I suspect, though, that Mr. Abram has carefully avoided broaching these nettlesome issues out of fear that by calling into question his born-again patriotism, he would thereby run the risk of losing his seat as the Administration's Judenrat.

Above all else, though, Abram's outrageous claim that I had, in fact, subverted Israel's interests struck me as being unaccountably naive: the almost mythical characterization of Israel as a political innocent in the woods, able to guarantee its existence on the basis of prophetic morality alone may play well in the American Heartland, but it doesn't do much for an 18-year-old Israeli recruit trying to improve his odds of survival against a coalition of enemy states possessing a nearly inexhaustible supply of manpower, Islamic fanaticism, petro dollars, modern Soviet and western armaments, and time. It would appear that salon Jews like Abram either can't comprehend or accept the unfortunate dichotomy that exists between the noble Halkachic values for which Israel stands and the unpalatable means she must sometimes use in order to survive. Assuming, on the other hand, that this grotesque display of obsequiousness on the part of Mr. Abram is motivated by his cowardly desire to somehow distance the American Jewish community from the artificially generated "fallout" of this affair, then he is forgetting that our strength as a race has traditionally come from standing united in defense of Klal Yisrael's spiritual and *national* interests whenever and wherever they have been threatened. Unlike Mr. Abram, Anne and I were raised with the belief that each and every Diaspora Jew should be willing to form part of what Ezra alluded to as a protective "wall of fire" around Israel because the notion that two communities could have mutually exclusive interests is an impossibility—we are one people, with one G-d, and are an indivisible land. That type of resolute solidarity as opposed to craven appeasement wins the respect of our adversaries amongst whom Caspar Weinberger should be counted as perhaps one of the most dangerous.

A friend of mine who happens to be a clinical psychologist has recently observed that the Secretary of Defense evidently suffers from what might be called a "Kreisky Complex," in which because of his Jewish ancestry, he has a strong unconscious need to distance himself from Jews and Israel. However, in light of the former Austrian Chancellor's rather conventional brand of Central European anti-Semitism, I would suggest that Caspar Weinberger's problem would more accurately be diagnosed as an "Amalek Complex," since he seems to despise Jews *more* than is absolutely necessary. It's illuminating to note in this regard Mr. Weinberger's publicly articulated preference for me to have been hanged. Apart from satiating his own pathological need for self denial, this gruesome outcome would presumable [sic] have also pleased both the Arab powers as well as their bureaucratic allies within this neurotic administration, whose barely concealed hatred of me is directly proportional to the value of the information made available to Israel. Having been denied the pleasure of seeing me swing from a gibbet in the local equivalent of Marjeh Square, Mr. Weinberger and his confederates at the Justice Department clearly intend to do whatever they can to demonstrate to their Arab friends that the Israeli agent and his wife are essentially dead in all but name only. Well, they can try to bury us alive but Anne and I are determined to survive if for no other reason than we don't want to give people like Mr. Weinberger and Prince Bandar the pleasure of having the final victory in this affair and thereby think that Jews lack the metal for self sacrifice. As Jews have a well established history of outlasting their persecutors, I can assure you that these two will do their utmost to maintain this aggravating racial habit.

These brave words aside, I am extremely worried about Anne's deteriorating medical condition at Lexington. The court was well aware of her precarious state of health when we were sentenced, since Anne had to be held up before the judge and needed the assistance of two nurses to make it through the proceedings. In spite of depositions from Anne's physicians clearly stating that incarceration would pose a grave threat to Anne's life due to the fact that no prison hospital was either equipped or predisposed to treat her extremely rare gastrointestinal disorder, the judge nevertheless indicated that she should have thought about those risks when she chose to put her loyalty to Israel and me above that of the "law." Predictably Anne' health has deteriorated at an alarming rate—she can no longer eat solid food and her weight has dropped to below 95 pounds. Although the FDA has indicated that it would not object if a drug currently available only in Western Europe were given to her, the Bureau of Prisons has adamantly refused to authorize this because of their opinion that Anne's crime "against" the United States precludes her from such unusual dispensations—even on humanitarian grounds. Despite her desperate need for periodic endoscopies, the prison has decided that she can wait until their schedule is not so busy. Since no one will permit my wife to have any pain medication, she spends most of her time in agony. Paralleling this outrageous medical treatment are a host of institutional abuses designed to exert maximum psychological pressure upon her, foremost amongst which is the censorship of our correspondence to the point where it's almost meaningless. Whoever is responsible for screening my letters to Anne is single handedly destroying the government's supply of magic markers since virtually everything is being blacked out ostensibly for "security" reasons. Even newspaper articles I send her pertaining to Israel arrive shredded. To add insult to injury, Anne was attacked several weeks ago by a deranged inmate. That, Mr. Cohn, is my wife's reality right now. It is not very pretty and is probably going to get much worse as time progresses and the Jewish community slowly forgets about her.

Anne's brutal treatment by the government at sentencing was all the more remarkable given the fact that she was never charged with having committed espionage and her "heinous" loyalty to me stands in marked contrast to the case of Mrs. Edward Lee Howard who, even though she facilitated her husband's defection to the Soviet Union, has not even been indicted for obstruction of justice, let alone conspiracy. It should also be kept in mind that as a direct result of Howard's escape, the CIA's covert operations group in Moscow has reportedly been rendered all but useless by a spate of executions and improved KGB security measures recommended by the renegade American intelligence officer. But Mrs. Howard not only remains free but is permitted to pay for her husband's credit card bills which he has generated while living in Russia! Is there a double standard in practice or am I missing something?

Although I don't know how the court will respond on July 3rd to our motions for a reduction of sentence, it's more than likely that Mr. Weinberger will mount a rather strenuous effort to have the original sentences sustained. If anything, his ill-advised advocacy of a pro-Iraqi tilt in United States policy towards the Persian Gulf War has only fueled his animosity towards me. Just a few weeks ago, in fact, Mr. Weinberger stated that in his opinion America's ability to defend the Arabian Peninsula's oil fields today have been irrevocably compromised by both the successful Iranian interrogation of William Buckley, the former CIA station chief in Beirut, as well as my activities on behalf of Israel which were somehow linked to the former tragedy. I suspect that lumping me in with the Iranians will be rather well received in the various Arab capitals where the portrayal of Israel as the moral equivalent of Khomeini's Islamic Republic has been a leit motif of their propaganda campaigns over the past six years. It would now seem that this invidious comparison has moved significantly "upscale" by being disseminated by no less a spokesman than the United States Secretary of Defense.

I'm sure that this new gospel will be avidly embraced by the presiding judge who reportedly told our lawyers just before we were sentenced that he wouldn't tolerate any "pro-Israeli" statements to be made in court since it was his opinion that Israel's treatment of the Palestinians could be unfavorably compared to Nazi atrocities during the Second World War. The judge is also furious over our continued refusal to repudiate our cause, which he is choosing to interpret as a blatant manifestation of "stiff-necked arrogance." Despite the fact that some people might attribute our uncompromising attitude to principle, that word doesn't have much currency in Washington these days, particularly if it's associated with Israel. Of course, I suppose it was a matter of "principle" that lay behind Weinberger's decision to let injured crewmen from off the USS *Stark* be treated in Bahraini hospitals even though back in 1983 when the Marine Barracks in Beirut was destroyed by a Shiite suicide bomber, he also claimed that it was a matter of principle which justified his adamant refusal to let Israeli hospitals treat the wounded, one of whom may very well have died as a result. It is therefore apparent that in Mr. Weinberger's code of ethics there are some principles which are even more important than the lives of injured United States servicemen. It is indeed ironic to realize that the principles which figured prominently in my decision to assist the Israelis may one day save a great number of American troops as well.

Perhaps in reaction to complaints being voiced by the Jewish community about the unjust nature of my sentence, the government appears set to unleash a stream of unattributable "leaks" designed to smear my reputation to the point where nobody would be willing to stand up for me. The authorities threatened this seventeen months ago when I refused to cooperate with them by implicating a truly remarkable list of prominent Jews in my activities. I wasn't asked for proof of their association with Israeli intelligence, mind you, just for a mark next to their name. You know, Mr. Cohn, there are two methods of silencing a person in my situation: one time honored technique is to have them meet with some violent end while in prison. A more sophisticated approach, developed into a high art by the experts of Dzerzhinsky Place, is to call someone's sanity into question while simultaneously slandering his character beyond repair. Accordingly, I'm preparing myself for a barrage of allegations concerning my drug addiction, alcoholism and mental stability—the "unholy trinity" as we call it in the disinformation business.

Although I fully intend to challenge these spurious and malicious charges in court, the damage will already have been done. Will anybody care to know in the wake of all the slander that I had been forced to go to a psychiatrist in an effort to have me resign after a special navy operation with which I'd been associated and turned sour? Will it matter that the psychiatrist had subsequently given me a clean bill of health and felt that the navy had been unethical for having abused his profession? Will people be outraged to learn that shortly after my arraignment the file containing my case history mysteriously disappeared from this psychiatrist's office? Now do you understand, Mr. Cohn, what my wife and I have been up against for the past nineteen months?

What am I supposed to do from prison when my former superior, a real mamser [sic] of the first order, claims that I was an "incompetent," while the record indicates that I've received two outstanding performance awards and a decoration from the Secretary of the Navy? What kind of credibility does this man have after lying to investigators that I had absolutely nothing to do with Middle East affairs, while a review of the pertinent records clearly shows that on at least two occasions I was sent as the navy's Middle East expert to interagency anti-terrorism conferences? Perhaps this man's attitude towards me can be explained by pointing out that he wanted to characterize the Israeli retaliatory strike against the PLO facility in Tunis with which I've been associated as "an act of state sponsored terrorism." One could hardly consider such a man to be an unbiased character reference!

Moreover, how could a person in my former position have been a drug addict of all things and remain undiscovered by the battery of blood and urine tests to which we were periodically subjected? It should come as no surprise, then, that I was able to pass all of the FBI polygraphs which pertained to drug abuse. Indeed, given the prosecutorial zeal of the government attorneys in this case, one would have expected them to have submitted to the court any evidence they had which could substantiate a drug related offense. Even though such material does not exist, the authorities have, nevertheless, permitted the "rumor" of my drug corruption to be propagated in the media where I end up tilting at windmills in my effort to refute these unsubstantiated allegations. As far as my purported alcoholism is concerned, this is simply an example of "creatio ex nihilo." In fact, the one person who has been responsible for providing the press with this bit of fiction now claims that he's been misquoted and that he barely knew of my existence when we attended Stanford together in the early 1970s.

It would seem that in the absence of any *facts* which even suggest that my activities damaged the national security of this country, certain people have evidently decided to.

Anne's brutal treatment by the government at sentencing was all the more remarkable given the fact that she was never charged with having committed espionage and her heinous loyalty to me stands in marked contrast to the case of Mrs. Edward Lee Howard who, even though she facilitated her husband's defection to the Soviet Union, has not even been indicted for obstruction of justice let alone conspiracy, to sensationalize my purported debauchery to the point where that becomes the entire focus of public attention. Although the actual motive behind this "diversionary" effort is not readily apparent to me, the only explanation apart from pure vindictiveness that seems logical is that the government wishes to ensure that I remain a constant source of deep embarrassment for both the Jewish community and Israel. It has even been suggested by David Biale, the director of the Center for Jewish Studies at the Graduate Theological Union in Berkeley, that this "agenda may well have something to do with the Iranian arms scandal, for it would be no surprise if the likes of Caspar Weinberger and Edwin Meese regard Israel as the main culprit in dragging Ronald Reagan's presidency to the brink of disaster. For the real and imagined crimes of Israel, then, [I] may well have been seen as a likely sacrificial scapegoat, a way of sending a message to Israel and perhaps to the American Jews "not to step out of place again." Certainly, everything Anne and I have experienced during this ordeal lends credibility to this ominous assessment.

Finally, in light of all the partisan furor surrounding the recently published Eban-Rotenstreich-Tzur reports, it would be appropriate for me to emphasize that my actions were not undertaken to enhance any particular Cabinet, government official or political party, but were prompted solely to guarantee the security of the Jewish state and people. I wasn't motivated by greed and I didn't set out to become a martyr. A situation simply developed that I just couldn't walk away from in good conscience. I do not condemn the cause I served, but only the cowardly leaders who decided to sacrifice us all on the twin altars of diplomatic and personal expediency. So be it. Perhaps these are the people for whom we should truly feel sorry because they will all one day have to explain their actions to a power far greater than any Knesset investigating committee. When all is said and done, though, Anne and I can only hope that the pronounced military advantage which Israel will now reportedly enjoy over her Arab and Soviet enemies lasts long beyond that point in time when our names are but distant memories—and that, as you know, Mr. Cohn, would indeed be sufficient compensation for any Jew. In spite of everything which has happened to us, we are still confident that the American Jewish community, if not its leaders, will one day conquer its fears and complexes long enough to correct the terrible injustice which has been visited upon our heads.

Best wishes,
Jonathan Pollard